COFFEE
HOW TO
BUY IT
HOW TO
BREW IT

JASON SCHELTUS

Smith
Street
Books

CONTENTS

INTRODUCTION

I started writing *Coffee: How to buy it, how to brew it* as an expansion to my first book, *Liquid Education: Coffee*, but I quickly found that my interest and passion lay in helping people better understand the coffee industry as a whole, not just coffee itself. As a result, this new book covers much more information about buying coffee, for all sections of the industry: the home-brewing enthusiast, the cafe owner buying wholesale roasted coffee, and the roaster selling wholesale roasted coffee.

In many ways, this book is a reflection of my role as a co-owner of Market Lane Coffee, based in Melbourne, Australia. I am very lucky to have an extremely varied and interesting job, which I have done for the last nine years. I travel to coffee-producing countries to buy green coffee several times a year, choosing particular coffees from producers that we have been buying from every year since we first opened Market Lane. I look for new coffees and new areas where coffee is grown, but, for me, the most rewarding part is talking to coffee producers year in and year out about how our customers enjoy their coffee. I have travelled to many countries, and my role in purchasing green coffee has ranged from choosing small micro-lots for Market Lane, to helping other roasters choose large lots and purchase these through Melbourne Coffee Merchants[1].

My role at Market Lane Coffee means I also set the pricing and control the costs for both our wholesale and retail businesses. Day to day this involves managing the costs, rather than looking at the revenue, but crucially it involves planning for increases in pricing and looking for ways to generate revenue. This unique view on the industry as a whole has given me a lot of perspective as to how it works, where the margins are and where we can improve.

In this book, I discuss how to choose coffee, both from a retail customer's point of view and from a cafe's perspective. I have paid particular attention to pricing, as I haven't seen this topic overtly tackled in other publications, the exception being Colin Harmon's recent book *What I Know About Running Coffee Shops*, which goes over the details of costing for coffee shops. I also cover some of the technical aspects of roasting and brewing, along with recommendations for efficiency when brewing in a cafe setting.

This book is for anyone who is interested in coffee or the coffee industry. I won't claim that it is the authority on the subject, but I do believe that it offers a unique perspective and covers some topics that have not yet been discussed. Australia has one of the most diverse cafe scenes in the world, driven largely by the enormous number of small businesses that operate in the sector. The largest company in the cafe and coffee-shop sector has only a 7 per cent share of the market[2], and it is competing with a huge number of small and medium businesses. Each of these businesses and their owners have had to find their way on their own, by trial and error, and many have failed while trying. Cafes and coffee wholesalers can be structured in many different ways, but some of the fundamentals (such as green-coffee pricing) are the same worldwide. I hope that this book can give these smaller businesses a little more insight into some of the strategies and pricing that can work, and help make them as successful as possible.

Note: In writing this book, I have become acutely aware of the variances in weights and measurements units used across the industry. To broadly explain their context, coffee was first traded internationally in USD per pound (USD/lb), and because it's still traded as an international commodity, this pricing is still used worldwide for everyone who trades coffee. But most countries have since switched to metric[3], so all day-to-day coffee producing is discussed in metric, as are the workings for most cafes. In fact, a lot of cafes in the United States will use grams rather than oz, because it is easier to use grams for small measurements such as dosing amounts for espresso and water.

---

1 Melbourne Coffee Merchants is owned by Fleur Studd and is run independently of Market Lane Coffee. Fleur also owns Market Lane Coffee jointly with me, so the two companies work together where they can. In particular, we share resources in purchasing green coffee, and some Market Lane Coffee employees assist Melbourne Coffee Merchants in tasting and purchasing from coffee-producing countries. You can read more about our relationship here: melbournecoffeemerchants.com.au/about-us/

2 Ibisworld Industry Report 2015.

3 Only the United States, Liberia and Myanmar have remained imperial.

BUYING

COFFEE

BUYING COFFEE FOR HOME

Selecting coffee to use at home can be difficult and sometimes intimidating. As with wine (and now craft beer), a lot of technical and marketing terms that aren't very clear are used. This section will shed some light on what information matters most when selecting coffee, and what information you can chalk up to marketing and disregard. There are a couple of certifications to look out for, but generally the coffee industry doesn't have any fixed standards when it comes to labelling for customers.

THE IMPORTANCE
OF TRACEABILITY

Until very recently, coffee was traded as a commodity, in a way similar to wheat, oil or gold. There were different grades for different origins based on quality, altitude and even the physical size of the coffee bean. Trading in this way made sense for a young industry. After all, how many roasters and customers could the world sustain? Well, a lot, as it turns out.

Improving coffee's traceability has become more of a focus for roasters only in the last 20 years, due to a desire for better-quality coffee for their customers and more consistent quality year to year. Coffee brokers and roasters started to look for individuals or groups of farmers who were interested in making improvements to their processes in exchange for a higher price. These improvements were often as simple as only picking ripe cherries, or only selecting lots for export from the highest parts of a farm (the ideal altitude for growing coffee is 1,500 m/4,920 ft above sea level), but the consequences were significant: changing coffee from a commodity to a traceable, quality product meant huge improvements for consumers, and better prices for coffee producers.

So how traceable does coffee have to be to make a difference? This is a difficult question to answer, because each coffee-producing country has a different socio-economic background and, therefore, a unique economic relationship between coffee producers, exporters and roasters. Poorer countries tend to have more government structure surrounding the export and trade of coffee, while more developed countries tend to have fewer mediating bodies.

In countries such as Ethiopia, Kenya and Rwanda, coffee co-operatives can be made up of thousands of members, each being a small family with only a few coffee trees to tend to and look after (one coffee tree can produce a few kgs/lbs of coffee per season). In circumstances such as these, traceability is generally limited to the larger co-operative name and the region in which the co-operative is based. In more developed countries such as Brazil, Guatemala or Costa Rica, vast coffee plantations can be owned by a single person or a single family, making traceability far more precise.

To make a difference to the lives of the producers, traceability needs to extend down to a washing-station level and, ideally, further. Traceability that extends only to a higher level, such as a whole region, has very little benefit.

MAKING INFORMED CHOICES

As with many products, knowing the source of coffee can help inform retailers and consumers about other issues they might care about. Having the ability to speak directly with coffee producers allows good roasters and retailers to gain insight into that producer's practices, which not only helps with quality assurance but also allows for transparency on two main ethical issues linked to coffee production: environmental concerns and exploitative labour practices.

Environmental concerns

The negative environmental impacts of coffee production can include waterway contamination, clear-felling of forests and the development of monocultures. The use of fertilisers is common in Central and South America (less so in Africa), and overuse or careless application can lead to the acidification of soil and waterways, killing native wildlife and negatively impacting biodiversity. All water runoff from coffee processing needs to be treated to kill any remaining bacteria or sugars, so as not to change the chemistry of the waterways in areas surrounding production.

The ethical implications of destroying local environments to boost crops are very serious; many communities rely on a healthy environment to produce subsistence crops, especially in the poorer parts of the world.

Exploitative labour

This is a grave concern in the coffee industry. The simple fact is that children under 14 years of age should not be working, whatever the circumstance. The issue becomes complicated by the fact that in places like Central and South America, it is predominantly indigenous people who make up the majority of the picking workforce, and sometimes they have travelled a long way for the work. In these cases, the children will travel with the family to the farm, and stay with their family while the parents work. It's tragic that these children will sometimes work with the family to pick or sort coffee, rather than go to school or childcare, and it requires efforts from all parts of the industry to ensure it comes to an end.

Without traceability, environmental degradation and workforce exploitation can go unchecked and uninhibited. With traceability, buyers and consumers can be empowered to make informed decisions about which products and producers to support. As regulation in the coffee industry is not yet tight enough to prevent these issues, retailers have a responsibility to make a difference with the choices they make, as well as a responsibility to communicate these choices – and the reasoning behind them – to their customers.

ROAST DATE

Good coffee retailers and roasters should only sell coffee for a short period after it has been roasted, so that you can enjoy it while it's fresh. Well-roasted coffee doesn't have to be consumed immediately for it to be at its best, but it should be consumed within 4–6 weeks of roasting. If you're buying coffee from a trusted retailer or roaster, and you know that they're careful about their stock age and rotation, then you don't need to check that the coffee is fresh every time you make a purchase. But if you're trying coffee from a new roaster, I would recommend checking that the coffee has been roasted within the last week. If there is no obvious roast date on the bag, it may be linked to a batch number that a staff member can help you with. If there is no roast date on the bag and no roast information available, it is safe to assume it was roasted months ago and, therefore, past its optimal flavour.

HARVEST INFORMATION

In most cases, coffee is only harvested once or twice a year. The harvest cycle for coffee is based on a flowering cycle and rain, so it's different in every country and even in different regions of the same country.

The altitude that the coffee is grown at will also affect the cycle, with coffees grown at higher altitudes flowering at a more consistent time of year than coffees grown at lower altitudes. On large coffee estates that have a wide altitude range, coffees grown in lower parts of the farm will be ready first, with coffees from higher parts being harvested later. As you can see, it's complicated.

The green coffee itself will taste best when roasted and consumed within 12–18 months of harvest. A good retailer or roaster will only sell coffee that has been harvested within this timeframe, but again, if you're buying from a retailer or roaster you don't know, the best thing to do is to ask whether their coffee is current crop or fresh crop – that is, any coffee that has been harvested in the last 12–18 months – and hopefully they can provide this information. The issue for roasters is that it's difficult to always maintain fresh crop coffee, because purchasing one year's worth of coffee from one particular country means that it has to last a whole year.

CERTIFICATIONS

There are a few certifications available to coffee producers for the benefit of the retail customer. The most common certifications are certified organic, Fair Trade, Rainforest Alliance and Cup of Excellence.

CERTIFIED ORGANIC

Internationally, there are many different associations that can administer organic certification, and different food labelling laws apply, too. If you want to support organic farming practices, it's worth noting that organic farming can exist without certification, but it's not all that common. Bolivia is one notable exception – their coffee industry is very small, and most of the producers have a special relationship with the environment, caring for it as if it were a whole living entity. Ethiopia is another exception; a lot of the coffee there is grown by individuals, a few plants at a time.

Australia has particularly lax labelling laws when it comes to labelling for organic practices. Unlike the United States or the United Kingdom, in Australia you can label anything as 'organic' even if it is literally dripping with fungicides and pesticides. If a food is labelled 'certified organic', however, it does have to conform to strict rules applied by a few associations, so always look out for a particular certification rather than just the word 'organic'.

FAIR TRADE

This guarantees a minimum price paid to coffee producers. It's currently USD $1.40 per lb for washed arabica coffee. This price is less than half the amount you would pay for high-quality coffee from specialty coffee shops around the world, and currently USD $0.25 per lb more than the current 'C' price (the global commodity price for coffee) for washed arabica coffee.

The Fair Trade price is a guaranteed minimum for co-operatives that qualify, but the certification does not assure buyers of any quality standards other than washed arabica. Choosing Fair Trade coffee over similar lower-quality coffees or commodity-traded coffees can be a good choice to ensure a better price is paid to producers, but if you are buying high-quality coffee then the price paid to the producer will be based on the quality rather than the commodity or Fair Trade price.

CUP OF EXCELLENCE

This is a national coffee quality competition held in a number of different coffee-producing countries each year. It is free for producers to enter, and they are only required to submit a small sample of their coffee. The competition is independently audited to ensure it is free from influence or corruption, which ensures buyers have confidence in the system. The best 30–40 coffees of that country for that year are determined initially by a national jury, and then finally by an international jury representative of international buyers. Once the final coffees have been ranked, the top coffees (scoring 85 out of 100 or above) are awarded Cup of Excellence, and then sold at auction over the internet. The starting price for these coffees is USD $5 per lb, and the auction drives the price up from that, usually to USD $8–15 per lb, but it has gone as high as USD $300 per lb, as in the recent Costa Rican Cup of Excellence.

The aim of the competition is to connect coffee producers with coffee roasters or brokers who have a common goal of high quality. The competition helps to build relationships between growers and roasters, while establishing and quantifying the value and quality of their coffee. This means that in years to come, whether the coffee is submitted to the competition or not, the producer can sell their coffee at a premium price based on its quality. If a bag of coffee has a Cup of Excellence sticker on it, you can be assured the quality has been checked many, many times, and a great price was paid to the producer.

BUYING COFFEE FOR CAFES

As is the case with purchasing coffee as a retail customer, I believe that transparency is extremely important when buying coffee for a cafe from a wholesale coffee roaster. If your coffee supplier can't tell you where the coffee is from or much about from where it was purchased, it leads to the conclusion that provenance is not very important to them. When provenance details of coffee are not shared, or are not transparent, it leads to the coffee being traded as a commodity.

This chapter is for cafe owners and managers, or anyone who wants to understand more about purchasing roasted coffee from wholesalers. Of course, there are many different pricing methods and quality choices you can make, and I am not suggesting what follows is the only, or the most correct, way for you, but more so presenting my experience and opinion.

GETTING STARTED

As a wholesale customer, you can request samples from multiple roasters, along with brewing recommendations and, of course, information about the coffee. One of the most challenging aspects to realise and understand is the seasonality of coffee, complicated by the fact that almost every coffee will age differently. So a great starting question for your supplier is, 'When did you first start roasting this particular coffee?' And, if they know: 'When did this coffee arrive in the country?' Up to three months is great; up to six months and you might expect there to be some ageing flavours coming into the cup; more than six months and the coffee is probably already too old.

Tasting the coffee is, of course, the best way to know if you would be happy to serve it to your own customers, but how, and with what brewing method? I would always recommend cupping coffees[1] side by side for perspective and to understand the differences between them. For example, if you are looking for a new espresso, ideally you would taste five or six samples from different roasters side by side, and immediately dismiss any samples that have taste defects. Rank them in terms of whether you like them, and in terms of whether your customers would like them, and taste the top ones as espresso. The cupping method is not ideal for espresso roasts, but it is still a very fast and effective way of comparatively tasting more than a couple of samples. Furthermore, espresso brewing can hide ashy flavours and textural components of the flavour, but cupping allows you to taste all of these faults very clearly.

A lot of cafes make the mistake of trying to choose coffees they think their customers will like. Of course it's important that customers like and enjoy the coffees that your cafe serves, but not pleasing everyone is a much better scenario than not knowing who your target customer is. I think it's better in the long term that your customers know and understand what your values are (whether they agree with them or not), rather than sending out a mixed message that does not convey your values or ideas. Market Lane receives a lot of criticism for not offering soy milk because it compromises the taste and texture of the coffees we serve, but we are willing to take that criticism, because it means our customers, and future customers, know that we have strict quality principles that override being popular, or satisfying every customer's order. So write out the values of your cafe, and stick to them when choosing coffees to sell.

---

1 Cupping is a uniform brewing method that does not utilise any filtration. A ratio of 12 g of coffee to 180–200 g of water is normally brewed in a bowl for four minutes with boiling water. After the four minutes, the crust of the coffee is broken, and as most of the coffee falls to the bottom of the bowl, the top remnants are cleared off. The resulting brew is then sipped from the top, using a bowl-shaped spoon. The ratio of coffee to water can be adjusted to suit your preferred brewing method; for example, if you prepare brewed coffee in your cafe at an extraction of 20 per cent, the appropriate brew ratio would be 11 g/180 g (at a palatable 1.2 per cent strength for cupping).

WHOLESALE PRICING

The margin charged by wholesalers for roasted coffee ranges from very small (10–15 per cent gross profit margin) up to 60 per cent gross profit margin[1]. The reason the gross profit margin varies so much is that the cost to produce roasted coffee varies so much. I touch more on pricing for roasting later but, essentially, commercial coffee can be roasted in small batches (as little as 5 kg) or in huge factories making tonnes every day. The cost of the green coffee itself also varies greatly, but it generally aligns with quality and, as with most foods, the very best is much more expensive than the very good.

COFFEE

I'm always really humbled when I travel to coffee-producing countries; I see coffee farmers working hard picking coffee by hand, one bean at a time. It takes 25 coffee cherries at a minimum to have enough for one cup of coffee, and I like to keep this in mind when thinking about pricing.

Wholesale coffee pricing varies greatly, depending on where you are in the world and what coffee you buy. But generally, the range for good-quality coffee is AUD $30–$40 per kg (USD $9–$14 per lb). In my experience, cafe owners obsess over this per kg price of coffee at the expense of quality and potential selling price. For example, what is the point of buying a pretty average Kenyan coffee for filter coffee at AUD $40 per kg, which you can then sell at AUD $4.00 per cup, when you could buy a spectacular Kenyan coffee at AUD $60 per kg and sell it at AUD $6.00 per cup?

---

1 Where the gross profit margin percentage is the percentage of the sale that makes up the margin. This is calculated by taking the sale amount minus the cost, and then dividing that by the sale price.

As you can see in the table below, the gross profit percentage is almost the same for both the cheaper coffee and the more expensive one, but, crucially, the gross profit dollar amount is a lot more for the more expensive coffee. And, more importantly, you are serving better coffee to the customer for a marginally higher price.

	Cost per cup (15 g)	Price per cup	Gross profit % per cup	Gross profit % per cup
Average Kenyan coffee	$0.60	$4.00	85%	$3.40
Spectacular Kenyan coffee	$0.90	$6.00	87%	$5.10

The same quality and price equation can be applied to espresso coffee, with similar results: a marginal increase in the price for the customer allows the cafe to purchase better-quality coffee.

It's hard to charge more than your competitors for a similar product, and understandably cafe operators push back on this concept. But new cafes charging the same amount as competitors without understanding the costs involved in their own business is a systemic issue. It will almost always cost a new business more than an established one to produce a similar product, due to depreciation costs, establishing costs and so on, so why aren't new cafes routinely charging more for their product?

The reason is often that cafes are opening in an already crowded market, so to entice customers to their new business, operators are competing on price and product quality, but doing so at a loss. In this way, new cafe operators are competing with established cafes at their own game, at their own quality level and at their lower price points. I'm not suggesting that you should increase prices for no reason, or that you should have higher prices just because your cafe is new. I am reasoning that, in my experience, customers are asking for better-quality coffee, and are happy to pay a premium to have it. Additionally, it is easier for new cafes to establish a higher baseline of quality than it is for established cafes to change to it.

Increasing prices in an established cafe is a difficult thing to do. It can upset some customers, and make them question the value of the coffee you serve. But also, in every scenario, the costs of running a cafe increase every year. Almost every expense line is affected by local increases, and unless the increases are passed on to your customers, they are absorbed by you. But there are ways to do it that will minimise upset to your customers.

- Be clear about price changes in advance. No one likes a surprise, and especially not when it comes to their daily habit. Give your customers a few weeks' notice that a price increase is coming, and be clear about what it is. Ensure that your staff are confident of the reasoning behind the change, and empower them to give away complimentary coffees to unhappy customers.

- Explain your reasoning. Rationally, your customers will be able to understand why you need to increase your prices, but in the moment their reactions will be emotional ones. So, find some data, write a few bullet points and explain clearly and honestly why you need to increase prices.

- Be open to feedback. Only one in 20 unhappy customers will communicate negative feedback to you, so make sure you are ready and listening when they do. In most circumstances, customers simply want what they had initially been promised, so consider this when dealing with complaints.

Following these steps, we have increased our prices every few years at Market Lane. Each time it is difficult, and each time we are apprehensive about how our customers may respond. We have found that as long as we are confident in the quality of our coffee and customer service, the price increase transpires with a minimal loss of customers.

The biggest increase we made in one go was in 2015, when we increased the price of our milk drinks from AUD $4.00 to $4.50, a 12.5 per cent increase. We hadn't increased our prices for five years, so we were nervous as to how this increase would be received. We worked hard to prepare our staff, giving them information about why we made the decision and how we justify our value to customers. When the increase came into effect, we saw a change in volume of less than five per cent in drink sales, but a 10 per cent increase in gross revenue across all our stores. This increase allowed us to keep buying the high-quality coffees our customers want, to keep our staffing levels high and ensure continued good customer service and, importantly, allowed us to keep delivering what we promise to our customers.

Waste

A lot of the discussions I have about pricing wholesale coffee involve me raising the topic of efficiency or, particularly, waste. In this case, the waste I am talking about is the amount of coffee that is bought by the cafe but then not sold on to customers for a range or reasons, which include:

- Dialling in the coffee in the morning
- Staff coffees throughout the day
- Kitchen staff coffees
- Grind adjustments throughout the day
- Mistaken orders
- Single or spare shots not being used
- Channelling shots, or poorly prepared shots needing to be remade
- Coffee used in training staff

I'm not suggesting that you no longer dial in the coffee in the morning, or that you ban your staff from drinking coffee throughout the day, but I think each of these actions should be evaluated and understood. We made a number of changes at Market Lane to reduce waste, and they weren't too draconian! For example, now when making grind changes, we've trained our staff not to 'purge' the grinder as they make the change and to only make very small changes. This means that our staff might make more changes throughout the day, but the coffee on both sides of the grind size adjustment is served. This has ended up saving a lot of time and coffee.

From a cost-saving perspective, the results can be huge. Consider that for a recipe that calls for 18 g of ground coffee, you should be able to sell 54.5 serves from 1 kg of coffee. If you look at this from a revenue perspective, any small change here can have a large impact. The potential revenue from 1 kg of coffee (selling only AUD $4.00 espressos) is AUD $218. Losing just six shots of coffee from 1 kg for staff drinks or mistakes, etc., you can easily see the revenue drop to AUD $192 per kg – a whopping $26 in lost revenue per kg. If a typical cafe is using 30 kg of coffee per week, this is almost AUD $780 in lost revenue.

The best way to monitor this change in revenue is by doing a stocktake each morning before service, over a few days, preferably on some busy and some quiet days. Then take all the coffee used during this period and divide it by the number of drinks sold. This is your baseline. Don't worry about accounting for extra shot orders or anything like that; this baseline will help you reduce wastage, and it doesn't really matter where you start. In most cases, this approach will help you reduce the amount of wholesale coffee you purchase by a few or even many kg per week.

In my experience, most cafes are locked into a selling price because of the market they are entering, and then only deal with profitability once they are established. But when you look at this logically, it makes no sense to operate this way. First you should establish what the cost to make your product is, then evaluate whether you can feasibly sell it at the 'market price'. Increasing sales volume and growing your business only makes sense when the model you are operating is profitable, or when your target size is profitable. But this requires an understanding of the costs involved.

MILK

Since the early 1900s, milk production has slowly become more industrialised. Milk from large dairies is highly processed – from splitting fat content down to tenths of a single per cent and reconstituting it, to homogenisation processes that alter protein structures and make digestion difficult.

In most western countries, milk sold through supermarkets for consumption is legally required to be pasteurised by heat treatment. The most common method is to heat the milk to a high temperature (around 96°C/205°F) for a very short time, which is known as flash pasteurisation. A more gentle method is to heat the milk to a lower temperature (around 65°C/150°F) over a longer time. This method is less harsh on the milk, and seems to result in a better flavour than flash pasteurisation.

Small-scale dairy farms tend to produce better-quality milk than larger-scale operations. When looking for a milk supplier, ideally look for certified organic milk that is preferably biodynamic, which ensures the soil and environment are closely considered when farming dairy.

Good pasture, the breed of dairy cow, and milk processing are the main factors that positively impact the flavour of milk. Cows should be fed a good variety of grasses and flowers; however in much of the dairy industry, cows are fed just one or two varieties of grain, which produces a very simple and bland milk. Holstein-Friesians are the world's most popular dairy cow due to their capacity for high milk production, but Jersey cattle are still fairly common and produce milk with a superior flavour.

The pricing of milk varies a lot depending where you are. In Australia, for example, the price of wholesale milk ranges from AUD $1–$2 per litre, which includes giant milk factories and small family-owned dairies with small herds. The amount of milk used for coffee drinks ranges from small 6 oz cups that contain just 90 g[1] of milk to 8 oz takeaway cups that can hold 180 g of milk. The amount of milk used in a drink obviously depends on the cup size, but it is also greatly affected by how it is textured – a cappuccino should have less milk than a cafe latte, because the latte is more thinly steamed. The price range means it's tempting for penny-pinching cafe owners to choose the cheaper milk, but as with the coffee, it can be a false economy. Without considering the amount of milk you're using to make the drinks you sell, the price is not the biggest issue. To establish a baseline of how much milk is being used per drink sold, do a stocktake each morning, then divide the number of litres of milk used by the number of drinks sold. As an indication, the last time I measured milk usage at one of our cafes, we were using 125 ml of milk per coffee drink sold. Note that this volume of milk includes all espresso-based coffees – black coffees and coffees with milk. If you can, divide the milk used only by the number of milk coffees sold and compare it to a theoretical average milk drink. This figure represents the true cost of the milk in your coffee. If you aim to reduce milk wastage, you will inevitably decrease this cost. As with any metric, as soon as you start reporting it, you will find that wastage decreases.

---

1 Whole milk weighs roughly 1.05 g/ml, so it is slightly denser than water, but I still find it really useful to measure how much milk is used in each coffee drink by weight. For example, our 220 ml cafe lattes contain 180 g (170 ml) of milk, while our cappuccinos contain 110 g (105 ml) of milk.

BUYING GREEN COFFEE

The wholesale coffee industry has changed a lot in the past 30 years. Historically, large cities would have a few roasters supplying coffee to local grocery stores and cafes, and these few roasters would buy coffee from a few green coffee brokers. Globalisation, as well as roasters looking to differentiate themselves from competitors, has meant that the number of roasters has skyrocketed. At last count, Melbourne had 85 different coffee roasters, excluding the 20–30 that are utilising co-roasting spaces.

A COMPLEX PROBLEM

The proliferation of roasters means that there is a lot more competition to sell coffee to cafes and directly to customers. While competition is normally a good thing, competition in a crowded market can be detrimental for consumers, as quality and value are often the first victims of price-cutting by wholesalers. Wholesalers in a saturated market will offer 'the same product' for a lower price to make switching to their brand more appealing for retailers. In turn, the wholesaler looks to cut their cost of production, and to do this the first aspect they focus on is the raw product cost. This means that consumers in a saturated market are paying the same price for lower-quality products, while retailers save on the difference.

I don't know what the solution to this is, but I do know that price-cutting is not it. After all, no matter how low your price is for what you're selling, there will be someone else in the market who can sell it at a lower price. So, by allowing the conversation (or sales pitch) to revolve around the minimum price that you can offer, you are allowing the price to be the main determining factor in a cafe's purchasing decision. Refocusing the conversation on what makes your coffee special, distinctive or better will allow you to halt the comparison of your coffee to other inferior coffees.

COFFEE VARIETIES

While there are only two main species of coffee plants grown commercially around the world, each one has a number of different varieties (or cultivars) that make up that species. These plants vary in height, shape, bean size, productivity, disease resistance and, crucially, flavour. Only since the 1980s has there been scientific research into the different characteristics and benefits of particular varieties, but even today it feels like our knowledge about the potential of coffee varieties is in its infancy.

ARABICA VS. ROBUSTA

The two main species of coffee grown commercially around the world are *Coffea arabica* and *Coffea robusta*. Both of these species are part of the larger group of plants called the Coffea genus, which, in turn, is part of the Rubiacea family (a family that also includes ornamental plants, such as gardenias). The main difference between arabica and robusta is their native origins and, therefore, what they are conditioned to. Many plants develop bitter-tasting alkaloids (such as caffeine) as a kind of natural pesticide. Arabica is originally from higher altitudes and cooler climates, which means far fewer pests and, therefore, much lower levels of those bitter alkaloids that you'll find in robusta, which thrives in warmer climates.

There are two key characteristics that cause the flavour differences between arabica and robusta:

• Caffeine (alkaloid) content: robusta has about twice as much caffeine as arabica.

• Sugar content: arabica has 50–80 per cent more sugars than robusta.

It's these differences that cause robusta to have more rough, harsh and bitter qualities, while arabica is more sweet and fruity.

Robusta is grown in many places around the world because of its hardiness and high yield, and because it's easy to grow at lower altitudes. It makes up around 40 per cent of the world's coffee exports, with major exporters being Vietnam, Brazil and Indonesia. Despite this, not that much is known about robusta, primarily because it's not grown for quality, and is mainly used for cheaper coffee products, such as instant or pod coffee.

The arabica species is a big family, with many different varieties. Commercially, there are about 150 varieties of arabica grown around the world, but only 30–40 of these make up most of the world's production. A shrub that prefers to grow in the shade of other trees, or in fairly dense forest, *Coffea arabica's* native habitat is along the edges of the Great Rift Valley, through southern Ethiopia to the eastern parts of South Sudan. Now genetic testing has revealed that arabica is a descendent of robusta – that it changed over time and developed into what we now know today as arabica.

Deforestation is a huge threat to native varieties, which is why researchers are collecting and cataloguing thousands of different arabica varieties from native forests, such as the Keffa and Yayu forests in south-western Ethiopia, in the interests of genetic preservation and future investment. In places like this, coffee production is actually playing a big role in conservation, because the production of coffee in these areas requires forest cover.

In order to select the arabica variety that best suits the growing region, areas should ideally be test-planted with a great number of different varieties, and the best-tasting, most high-yielding variety should be the one chosen for that area. (This method has been applied recently in Rwanda and Kenya, with great results. Scott Laboratories in Kenya selected two varieties that are suited to Kenya's rich volcanic soils, and they produce a very distinctive coffee with blackcurrant and plum flavours.)

The reality of the way most varieties have ended up where they are, however, has more to do with chance than science. The history of coffee is extremely clouded with myths and stories, but what we do know is that coffee originated in Ethiopia, somehow made its way to the region that is now modern-day Yemen, and was then spread around the world by Dutch and English colonists. It's said that around the 1850s, a single plant variety called 'typica' was taken from Yemen and spread all over the world, with a few plants eventually mutating into a higher-yielding variety that was called 'bourbon'. It's a neat story, but in all likelihood, plants and seeds from many different varieties were probably taken from Yemen and Ethiopia to places like Brazil and Indonesia between 1820 and 1900.

Old coffee farms in early coffee-producing countries, such as Indonesia and Brazil, tend to be planted with what look like one of two 'heirloom varieties' – the first being bourbon, and the second looking and tasting more like typica. Over generations, these varieties have slowly mutated to adapt to the climates and soils of their new surroundings, meaning an 'original' bourbon variety that has grown in Indonesia for many years is now somewhat different to the same variety growing in Brazil.

Now farmers are able to use these mutations to their advantage, creating new varieties to better suit their needs. A good example is a variety called 'caturra', a mutation that was found in a field of bourbon plants in the Minas Gerais region of Brazil between 1915 and 1918. This new mutation had shorter nodes on the branches between the leaves and flowers. This shortening of the nodes meant that this particular plant was able to produce more flowers and, therefore, more fruit than a normal bourbon coffee plant. The plant was propagated separately and a new variety was born.

GEISHA

Geisha is arguably the world's most famous coffee variety, fetching huge premiums for its unusual and special taste. It began as an experimental planting on a farm in Panama, and is now planted widely (with varying success) around the world's coffee-growing regions. When it first emerged onto the market in the 2004 Best of Panama auction, it was clear this coffee variety was different to all others being commercially produced around the world; it was intensely floral, sweet and delicate. Because of its unusual qualities and small yields, it was immediately highly sought-after – and extremely expensive.

As an example of how unexpected and special it was in 2004, the highest bid in the 2003 Best of Panama auction was just over USD $3.00 per lb. Then, in 2004, the first 100 per cent geisha variety from Hacienda Esmerelda sold for a huge USD $21 per lb!

Since then, many coffee producers around the world have attempted to grow geisha, with some producing fantastic results and others struggling to produce a clean (and ripe) lot of coffee. To say that the Peterson family, the owners of Hacienda Esmerelda, are lucky or just hit the jackpot, is unfair. Many factors needed to fall into place to produce such a special coffee, but I think hard work and a commitment to excellence is the most important. Since 2004, the price for geisha varieties has continued to increase. Most recently, auction lots have skyrocketed to USD $800 per lb! Is this variety 200 times better than the best lots from a Guatemalan Cup of Excellence competition? If you are lucky enough to drink a cup of this variety, do you enjoy it 200 times more? Ultimately, these questions are irrelevant, because for people who can afford the luxury, the price or value is not a huge factor in the decision-making.

GREEN COFFEE PRODUCTION

It seems like there should be more knowledge and science behind the picking and processing of green coffee, especially when compared to other foods and beverages (like wine). But in most cases, when I visit a washing station or wet mill (where the coffee cherry is turned into a seed, or coffee bean), the process is very rudimentary and not particularly scientific. I think this is due to a number of factors, with cost of infrastructure and knowledge perhaps the main players. But I imagine that if increased worldwide communication continues, the resulting growth in coffee production knowledge will hopefully lead to more advanced processing techniques.

PICKING

Throughout the life cycle of coffee, quality can only be preserved, rather than improved or induced. This means that the quality of the coffee you drink at the end of the chain can never be higher than the quality of the cherry that's harvested. Ripeness plays a huge part in quality, so it's extremely important that the cherries are picked at the right time.

Even on farms with little or no change in altitude or soil, there is still some variance when it comes to the ideal time to pick each of the cherries, with the amount of ripe cherries on the farm increasing gradually, depending on their age or size. Apart from ripeness, producers have to consider other factors when it comes to picking cherries, including cost and availability of labour, the physical size of the farm, and expected revenue. One or more of these factors tends to be compromised in order for the producer to get the best outcome.

Sorting through ripe and unripe coffee cherries, Kiambu, Kenya.

PROCESSING

To store and roast coffee, the seed, or coffee bean, needs to be separated from the flesh and skin of the coffee cherry. Once it has been removed, it can then be dried for storage and transported to coffee roasters.

'Processing' refers to the way the coffee bean is removed from its fruit and how it is dried for export. This can be done in a great number of ways, and every country or region has its own method. Traditionally, these methods are determined by how much water is available to the processors at the washing station, and the methods are broken down into three broad categories: natural, washed and pulped natural.

Natural

The original and simplest method of drying coffee. After the coffee cherries are harvested from the trees, they are simply laid out to dry in the sun. This method suits producers in places that have very little in the way of processing infrastructure, such as Ethiopia and Indonesia, and is the most common way that growers process coffee for their own families. The issue with this method is that it's difficult to control the rate and extent of fermentation due to factors such as ambient temperature and rain. Natural process coffee can taste extremely fruity or winey, especially as it comes close to over-fermenting. This process can be used to produce lower-cost coffee, as in Ethiopia or Brazil, for example, but it can also be done carefully to produce exciting new flavours in coffee. Achieving an even and slow fermentation in whole coffee cherries is difficult, and to do it well requires control over the environment where the coffee is being dried. If the coffee gets wet, or dries too fast, it is spoiled. Recently, greenhouses have been used both to protect coffee during the drying process and to control the ambient temperature. One benefit of natural process coffee is that no water is used to process it, so it is traditionally utilised in areas that have a particularly dry period after harvest, or where water is scarce.

Natural process coffee drying at Finca Santa Clara, Guatemala.

Washed

The washed method was developed in order to reduce spoilage – common to the natural process method – and, therefore, increase the value of the coffee for producers. It begins with pulping, which is a mechanical method of removing the skin and some of the fruit. To then remove the small amount of fruit still attached to the seed, the pulped coffee is left in open tanks (sometimes covered with water) for 24–72 hours, during which time the excess flesh is fermented away. The beans are then rinsed and transported to drying patios. The fermentation time varies based on climate, as warmer temperatures lead to faster fermentation. The washed method produces a very clean flavour, but quite a mild texture and a lighter body compared to pulped natural or natural process coffees.

New machines called eco-pulpers are starting to become popular among coffee producers. These machines use less water than traditional pulpers, and have the added benefit of mechanically removing the leftover fruit from the coffee seed. The benefit of doing this mechanically, rather than with fermentation, is that large amounts of water can be saved and perhaps used elsewhere. Another reason producers are turning to eco-pulpers is that traditional fermentation methods contaminate water with sugars, which then need to be removed from the water before it is returned to waterways. This cleaning process is not always done, or is done insufficiently, so contamination of waterways (usually at the top of river systems) is unfortunately common in coffee-growing regions. Eco-pulpers reduce this environmental damage because they use very little water to process the coffee.

Washing coffee after fermentation, Kenya.

Pulped natural
The pulped natural process is used quite widely throughout Central and South America, especially in Brazil, where the huge volume of coffee production

means that the tank fermentation used in the wash method is not practical. Pulped natural, as it sounds, sits right in between the other two methods: the coffee cherry is pulped mechanically and then laid out to dry, without a washing or fermenting step. This method can result in a balance of heavy body and pleasant sweetness, and a cleaner flavour compared to natural process coffees.

While these are the three general categories for processing, every country and region has endless variations on these methods, depending on rainfall, climate and economy.

DRYING

Drying is a hugely important part of the coffee production process: it stabilises the beans for shipping, allowing coffee to be sold internationally. Without drying we would not be enjoying coffee from Africa and Central America for significant portions of the year. For export, coffee needs to be dried to a maximum moisture content of 12 per cent.

There are many ways for freshly processed coffee to be dried, but they can be broadly categorised into passive and mechanical drying.

Passive drying

Historically, this is the most popular method of drying coffee. Coffee is laid out to dry in the sun and raked several times a day so that it dries evenly. Passive drying generally takes up to 10 days. In regions that have minimal infrastructure, or do not export their coffee, this drying might be done on straw mats, bitumen roads or simply on the ground. This can lead to inconsistent drying, and the coffee can easily be contaminated with stones, sticks or dirt. Larger-scale producers in countries such as El Salvador and Guatemala construct drying patios – large, flat open spaces usually built from concrete – on which the coffee is spread out to dry. Patio drying still poses the same contamination problems, however, and it takes up a huge amount of space (on a 25 m²/269 ft² patio, it's only possible to dry about 180 kg of processed coffee at a time).

For export, producers work hard to increase the quality of their coffee so they can get a better price. Over the last 10 years, producers have found that drying the coffee on raised drying tables increases the airflow around the coffee, leading to more even drying and less spoilage or over-fermentation. Even better results have come in the last five years from stacking these tables into a type of shelving system and housing the drying units in a greenhouse with an openable roof and sides, allowing the producer to control the climate inside the greenhouse. This method also has the great benefits of reducing contamination and conserving space.

Drying beds, Moredocof, Ethiopia.

Mechanical drying

Mechanical drying is done when there is a lack of space to dry the coffee, or when the huge volume of production means that the coffee needs to be dried quickly. Mechanical dryers are usually large drums with perforated walls, and can be up to 4 m (13 ft) in diameter and 20 m (66 ft) long. The drums turn, agitating the freshly pulped coffee as hot air is blown through.

Mechanical drying has to be done carefully with constant monitoring, as there is a risk of over-drying, drying too quickly or browning – any of which can be disastrous as they will likely ruin hundreds of kgs (or lbs) of coffee. The air temperature needs to be kept quite low (around 40°C/105°F) and the airflow quite high, so the heat is distributed evenly. Drying at this temperature takes around 24 hours per batch and the heat source is generally a furnace powered by off-cuts from shade and coffee trees.

Not every mill will have mechanical dryers, but they are popular in a variety of countries, including Brazil, Bolivia and Guatemala. Since they are a large piece of infrastructure, dryers are limited to countries that can afford to run and maintain such large machines.

In general, mechanical drying results in an inferior flavour compared to passive drying. It's therefore common for mechanical dryers to be used in combination with passive drying, especially in places where it can take a long time to achieve the exportable minimum moisture content. For example, a mill might dry coffee on patios for five days until it's down to a moisture level of 20 per cent, and then finish the drying in a mechanical dryer to achieve an even level of 12 per cent moisture.

PRICING

Any discussion on pricing for green coffee is usually kept discreet, or secret, and I think there are a few reasons for this. The main reason is that the price paid for green coffee by roasters is surprisingly low compared to the price paid for coffee in a supermarket or cafe. Seeing that only 20 per cent of the roasted coffee price is paid as the export price from a producing country can be confusing and alarming in some cases[1]. While the export price of green coffee varies a lot, the fact is that it is only ever a small portion of the roasted coffee price. Without an understanding of the whole coffee supply chain, it's difficult to rationalise the pricing structure, which is why pricing is kept from end consumers of coffee. I hope to demystify the supply chain and make the pricing structure of coffee clear in the following section.

Historically, coffee has been traded as a commodity. While this has offered some structural stability to the industry, on the whole it has not been as beneficial to coffee producers as it has been to consumer countries and traders. I will discuss the price (technically the 'C-Price', or 'Futures C-Price') in $USD per lb (453 g) of coffee, as this is how coffee has been traded since the 1960s, and how it continues to be traded.

The price of coffee has had a number of historic highs and lows, but overall, the price paid to producers has decreased over time. The price spikes are usually only for short periods (when there are shortages of coffee in stores due to large weather anomalies, such as drought or frost), but the price lows typically last for extended periods. The long-term average price of coffee is $1.07 per lb, with a low of $0.42 in 2001 and highs of $3.00 in 2011.

---

1 An example of transparent but confusing pricing could be made with corn flakes. If I said that corn costs USD $0.15 per kg (USD $0.24 per lb), but corn flakes cost USD $8.90 per kg (USD $14.55 per lb), you would be surprised because about 90 per cent of corn flakes is corn. But as is the case with coffee, there are a number of complicated factors that determine the price of corn flakes, not just the price of the raw ingredients.

The cost to grow coffee itself ranges widely, depending on the amount of automation involved, the scale of the operation and the country of origin. Large-scale farmers in Brazil report that they can produce export-grade green coffee at $1.03 per lb, while the cost of production for Guatemalan coffee farmers is closer to $1.80 per lb for high-quality green coffee. This is the cost of all the inputs into the coffee, including the cost of land financing, seeds, fertiliser, wet processing, dry processing and labour throughout the process.

The prices paid to coffee growers can also vary hugely. Paying a sustainable price for coffee is an enormous issue; for example, over the past eight years, the total coffee production in Bolivia has dwindled from 70,000 × 60 kg bags per year down to just 30,000 × 60 kg bags per year. Some of this decline can be attributed to adverse weather conditions and political influences, but the underlying issue is that the income derived from growing coffee in Bolivia is not enough to keep producers motivated to continue. Landholders are switching to more profitable cash crops, such as coca, or simply moving to the cities to find service work.

The future will become more and more difficult for coffee producers if the futures commodity price keeps trending downwards. As an industry, we need to ensure that current coffee producers are paid well enough to not only meet the costs of coffee production but to improve their lives and, in many cases, raise them out of poverty.

Determining the price that is paid to a coffee producer is complicated by the fact that the industry in each country is so different. To outline the large variation between countries, let's look at two examples of the path that coffee takes. First, a transparent trade, as direct as possible in Ethiopia and, second, a transparent trade as direct as possible in Guatemala.

ETHIOPIA CASE STUDY

In the case of Ethiopia, the outgrower is a small landholder who supplies a local wet mill with coffee cherry. In many instances, these outgrowers are supported financially by the wet mill, via membership in a co-operative or simply by virtue of the wet-mill owner seeing the benefits of supporting local growers.

Commonly, the outgrower will sell their cherry to the wet mill, receiving up to 18 Ethiopian birr per kg ($0.65 per kg) of coffee cherry[1]. The coffee that's delivered has to meet a minimum quality level, determined visually by the mill as the cherry is delivered, and based on the amount of contamination of unripe cherries or leaf litter, etc. The quality of the cherry supplied can be used to determine the price – at this stage the wet mill may select certain lots to go into a premium selection. Or, more typically, the price paid to the outgrower is determined by the demand for cherry in the area, driven by the external price of coffee at the time.

The wet mill processes the coffee, dries it and then sells it on to the coffee union that represents it – the Sidama Coffee Union, for example. At this stage, the coffee is in a fairly stable 'parchment' form – completely dried to an export level, but remaining in its protective parchment skin[2], which allows it to be stored for a long time. In this form it's common for coffee to be stored for months before it is dry-milled and prepared for export.

It's during this time that the coffee is purchased, either by a coffee broker, an importer/roaster or an exporter. Once the coffee is contracted and purchased, it is then sent to be milled and prepared for export. The most direct transaction in Ethiopia is when coffee is bought from the Union itself, but any number of variations on this transaction can take place. For each step of this transaction, a margin or fee will be added to the price of the coffee. It's for this reason that the price paid by importers can vary greatly; the coffee could pass through a number of organisations before being milled and ready for export.

The price of Ethiopian coffee depends on numerous factors, including quality, volume and purchase method (the use of an exporter). But as an example of what portion of the selling price goes where for high-quality coffee, see the following breakdown:

---

1 Approximately 6 kg of coffee cherry is required to produce 1 kg of clean, exportable green coffee.

2 Approximately 1.5 kg of parchment coffee is required to produce 1 kg of clean exportable green coffee.

Stakeholder in process	Price paid to stakeholder ($USD/lb)
Outgrowers, farmers	$1.50 – $1.80
Co-operatives	$0.80 – $1.40
Unions	$0.40
Exporters	$0.30
F.O.B (Freight on Board) price:	**$3.00 – $3.90**

This example pricing breakdown refers to high-quality coffee, and only represents a very small portion (albeit an expanding one) of Ethiopia's export market.

Let's compare Ethiopia to Guatemala, a country with a very different history of coffee production, social conditions and labour costs. It's an interesting comparison because the two countries are so different, both culturally and in their approach to coffee production and exporting.

GUATEMALA CASE STUDY

Unlike Ethiopia, Guatemala has a much higher proportion of larger-scale landholders; approximately 40 per cent of the coffee production comes from medium- to large-sized landholders (above 2 ha/5 ac in size). The government also allows producers to export their own coffee, although in practice this is only feasible for producers who farm more than 5 ha (12 ac), and only common among producers that farm more than 10 ha (25 ac).

Producers farming 10 ha (25 ac) of coffee or more will usually wet-process their coffee at their farm, dry it and store it in parchment until it is ready for sale. At this point it will be processed by a dry mill, bagged and sorted, and exported. A typical coffee-buying transaction in Guatemala contains these very few intermediaries, and the most direct trade will be between the coffee producer and the importer/roaster.

While there will still be dry-milling and logistics costs involved, a lot more of the process from the cherry to export-ready coffee is undertaken by the coffee producers themselves.

Stakeholder in process	Price paid to stakeholder ($USD/lb)
Landholder/exporter	$1.80 – $4.00
Miller/exporter	$0.20 – $0.80
F.O.B (Freight on Board) price:	**$2.00 – $4.80**

LOGISTICS

Shipping coffee in small amounts from any producing country is problematic. The coffee trade has historically been very large in scale, with transaction sizes of Full Container Loads (FCL) being standard rather than small lots of tens of bags. It's predominantly these historical reasons that make shipping micro-lots expensive and difficult. Shipping an FCL from a few coffee-producing countries per year necessarily means that the roaster or importer needs to have the capacity to use or sell up to 3,000 × 60 kg bags per year, ruling out access to this for micro-roasters. But the larger problem with purchasing container loads of coffee direct from origin is financing. Purchasing an FCL of coffee costs anywhere between USD $85,000 and $160,000 for the coffee alone, plus USD $2,000–$4,000 in shipping costs and USD $2,000–$4,000 in clearance and taxes. For a business to purchase ten of these per year means that a large amount of capital is required; potentially one-quarter of the total yearly capital needs to be available at a time.

Purchasing coffee in a Less than Container Load (LCL) is possible, but when purchasing from more than one mill or exporter, a consolidator is required, and the fees associated with this can be large. Additionally, containers aren't shipped by weight, so there's no discount for a half-full container load – the shipping price is the same whether there are 300 bags in the container or 30. As direct trade has become more popular, and the use of green-coffee brokers has become less fashionable, the techniques and methods of shipping small amounts of coffee around the world are being tested more and more.

It's possible to airfreight coffee, but it's prohibitively expensive and an environmental disaster, especially when compared to sea freight, which is the most environmentally friendly transport method available. The table below shows the CO_2 emissions and cost of each transport type.

Transport type	CO_2 emissions (g/metric ton/kg)	Cost worldwide (USD/kg)
Sea freight	1–40 g	$0.22
Truck freight	60–150 g	$0.13 (per 100 km)
Air freight	500 g	$6.00

The costs associated with these types of freight are approximate, and will vary depending on location, etc. But as you can see, if we were required to account for the carbon emissions, it would make air freight even more expensive!

WHAT IS 'SPOT' COFFEE?

'Spot' is a term used for purchasing green coffee in a consumer country, where the price encompasses all expenses up to the point of sale. Practically, this means that coffee is held in a warehouse ready for a roaster to use, and they can purchase this coffee and start using it straight away. It's mainly used by roasters that don't have access to the scale and financing that would enable them to purchase coffee directly. It has been unfashionable, ever since a few roasters started marketing direct trade as a better way to purchase coffee. Most of the criticisms of spot coffee purchasing are not related to the principle or the process, but rather based on certain experiences and rumours. There is also the myth that the 'middle man' is always a bad thing, and should be cut out at all costs. Of course, there are situations in which intermediaries are not very useful and certainly sometimes exploitative, but these should be treated on an individual basis, rather than ruling out the option entirely.

Some benefits of purchasing 'spot' are:
- Risk of quality drop is mitigated, as this risk is absorbed by someone else
- Capital requirements are minimal
- Coffee is tasted and purchased in a finished condition

With the right purchasing partner, you can purchase spot coffee while also enjoying these benefits:

• The choice to support social programs that directly benefit a community

• The ability to buy the same coffee year in year out

• Opportunities to visit the farm and meet the producers

While it's common to categorise green-coffee purchasing into two camps – direct trade and spot purchasing – the truth is that there is a lot of crossover, and indeed room in between the two methods for a more tailored approach. As outlined above, it's possible to access some of the benefits of direct trade (closer relationships, supporting social programs, etc.) while reducing exposure to risk by using a broker. Neither approach is wrong and, in my opinion, one is not superior to the other.

SAMPLE ROASTING

Sample roasting is used at a few stages in the green coffee-buying process. It's often mistaken for a 'trial roasting' mechanism, incorrectly assuming you can devise a suitable roast profile on a sample roaster and then apply it to a commercial roaster. This is not possible due to a number of reasons, and is also beside the point. The objective of using a sample roaster is to produce roasted coffee to a standard that allows the purchaser or seller of the green coffee to determine its inherent quality (or potential quality). To evaluate a number of samples side by side, the quality of roasting has to be very consistent across the samples so the roast does not impact on the results of the cupping. There are similarities to commercial roasting, in that the sample roaster needs to have enough burner power and airflow to adequately roast the coffee in an appropriate time. But since the batch sizes on sample roasters are much smaller, sample roasters are usually specified with the appropriate levels of power and airflow. Issues with lack of airflow do commonly arise, although most of these are caused by ducting and fans being dirty.

BUYING GREEN COFFEE

ROASTING
COFFEE

Roasting coffee is a difficult skill to master. The fact that most people will only use one or two types of roasters in their career, and the fact that almost every roasting machine is unique, with its own tics and eccentricities, means that even the most skilled coffee roasters have a very focused and specific approach to it. This also makes it very difficult to teach roasting, because you can show someone 'how to roast' on a particular machine, but teaching them how to approach roasting on their own machine means that much more general information needs to be provided.

There's been a lot written about roasting already; two titles I would recommend are Scott Rao's *The Coffee Roaster's Companion* and Rob Hoos' *Modulating the Flavor Profile of Coffee*. I agree with a lot of what these two authors have to say about roasting, and I won't pretend to cover as much as they have, but I'll offer my perspective in addition to their work.

EQUIPMENT

The process of roasting itself is very simple: coffee is heated, browned, then cooled. The magic happens in the details of this process, and indeed the details of the equipment you choose, how it is set up, and how you approach roasting.

Large factory roasters tend to be designed fit for purpose, and usually as part of a whole plant (with green coffee cleaners, silos, blenders, etc.) rather than just the roaster on its own. If you have one of these, or are considering investing in a plant, I'd recommend engaging a consultant (in addition to the machine manufacturer) for your specific needs. A whole plant can cost anywhere up to several millions of dollars, so you need room in your budget to plan it well.

More common are shop roasters, classed as any roaster with a capacity of roasting up to 60 kg of coffee. Shop roasters were originally designed to be more compact and visually appealing, with a lower overall production capacity and the ability to be operated in smaller spaces and in view of the public. Today, there is still a clear distinction between shop roasters and factory roasters in their design, appearance and use, and the technology has changed very little since the early 1900s. In fact, with the exception of huge coffee-roasting plants, all roasters work from the same simple design: a cylindrical drum where coffee is agitated while being heated by hot air and/or a direct flame. The process is as follows:

- Coffee is weighed out and loaded into the hopper.
- Once the roaster has been preheated to a set temperature, the coffee is dropped into the drum.
- The coffee is heated by adjusting the gas pressure.
- Within 9–15 minutes, the coffee rises in temperature from room temperature to around 210°C (425°F).
- When the batch is done, the operator opens the door and the coffee spills out into the cooling tray.
- Room temperature air is pulled through the bed of coffee to cool it down, and within 4 minutes it is ready to be packed.

STAGES OF ROASTING

Coffee goes through some big physical changes during the roasting process and some important chemical changes that increase the flavour potential. It isn't possible to make a coffee brew out of dried, unroasted beans – they need to be dried to an even lower moisture content – and the coffee flavour as we know it is created by a browning process, as described below.

FIRST CRACK

As heat is applied to the green bean by air or from the drum walls, the moisture is forced away from the heat source, inwards towards the centre of the bean. As this happens, the outer edges of the bean start to become more brittle as they dry. Some light browning of the coffee starts to occur when the outside temperature reaches around 160°C (320°F). This drying of the outer layers of the bean creates a temperature difference between the surface of the bean and the moisture front. During this period, when the temperature is between 160°C (320°F) and 180°C (350°F), the pressure inside the bean increases until the bean fractures open slightly, releasing energy in the form of sound and heat. As the coffee approaches this point, called 'first crack', the heat being applied is lowered, so that the rate of temperature increase slows down and the coffee doesn't get scorched. However, if the pressure increase takes too long, the beans' cells do not expand enough during first crack, causing the coffee to brown unevenly.

BROWNING

The browning stage consists of eight different processes or degradations, but the main two are caramelisation and the Maillard reaction. Caramelisation begins around 160°C (320°F), but on its own it does not influence the flavour of the coffee a great deal. Most of this work is done by the Maillard reaction, which happens between 160°C (320°F) and the end point of the roast.

The Maillard reaction is a chemical reaction that occurs between amino acids and sugars when heat is applied to the bean, browning the coffee and producing more than 800 different aromatic compounds, resulting in the complex aromas we associate with coffee.

The challenge when it comes to roasting is that every coffee bean is different. Country of origin, growing altitude and coffee variety all play a part in distinguishing one bean from another, and differences in size, shape, density and moisture content, etc., mean that each coffee type requires a slightly different roast profile to get the most out of the coffee.

The most common challenge that roasters face is that their equipment limits the changes they can make through the roast. This is usually because the machine they are working with is under-powered for its specified rating, or because the power output is linked to the airflow, which limits the energy input options.

WHAT ARE YOU MEASURING?

When talking about the stages in the roast, or the different points during the roasting process, we talk about the bean (or bean pile) temperature. But what is this, and how is it measured? The bean temperature is measured with a thermocouple (a type of temperature sensor), which aims to measure the outside temperature of the beans as they are being roasted. Maximising the contact the thermocouple has with the beans and minimising the contact it has with the roasting air is key, so the ideal placement for the thermocouple is the place in the drum where there are the most beans for the most amount of time. On a drum roaster that rotates clockwise, the ideal placement can be seen on the opposite page.

Commonly, roasters will have this thermocouple misplaced, and will be measuring too much of the roasting air temperature, thinking that it is the bean temperature. The trouble with this is that for most of the roast, the roasting air temperature should be significantly more than the bean temperature – up to 70°C (160°F) more. So even a moderate influence of the roasting air on the bean pile thermocouple will have dramatic impacts on the taste.

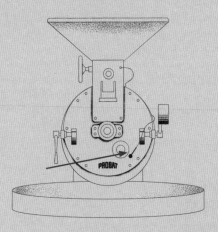

Thermocouples come in various types and sizes. The two most commonly used in roasters are K-types and RTD types, which differ slightly in the way they measure temperature, range, response time, and accuracy. RTD types are more common in larger roasters, a preference based solely on the fact that they are more durable than other thermocouple types; K-types are actually better for roasting because they have a faster response time than RTD types.

The diameter of the thermocouple also influences its response time, so I recommend a 3 mm diameter thermocouple for most roasters up to 60 kg, and a thicker (more durable) thermocouple for larger machines. The response time is important, particularly at the end of the roast when seconds in development time can count. Response time is also useful in environmental thermocouples when assessing how effective gas changes have been.

POWER OUTPUT

There are many different (and confusing) units of measurement used when talking about the power output and energy consumption of coffee roasters. In the table on the following page, I attempt to explain some of these terms in reference to roasters.

kW	Kilowatt	A unit of power, used to define the output of a burner or motor.
kWh	Kilowatt hour	A unit of energy, defined as 1 kW used during one hour. For example, a 1 kW motor running for one hour will use 1 kWh of energy.
BTU	British Thermal Unit	A unit of heat, defined as the amount of heat required to raise the temperature of 1 lb of water by 1° Fahrenheit.
m³/hr	Cubic metre per hour	A unit of gas consumption, defined as one cubic metre of gas per hour. When the type of gas is known, this can be used to calculate the power output of the burner.
MJ	Megajoule	A unit of energy, equal to one million joules, approximately 0.3 kWh.
MJ/hr	Megajoule per hour	A measure of gas consumption or energy consumption. Can be used to calculate power output in kW, but it's not a perfect equation.
kPa	Kilopascals	A measure of gas pressure. It's very important for roasters to be hooked up to the correct line pressure.
V	Volts	A measure of electrical potential difference. Sometimes more easily understood as the water pressure in a pipe.
A	Amp or Ampere	A measure of electrical current. In the water pipe analogy, amps would be the volume of water flowing through the pipe.
W	Watt	A measure of power, volts multiplied by amps.

Roaster manufacturers specify the capacity of their machines in kg of coffee, either by batch or in output per hour. For example, the Probatone 60 would have the theoretical output of 240 kg per hour: 60 kg capacity × 85 per cent (accounting for 15 per cent weight loss) × 4 (four batches per hour). This is based on the assumption that the machine can adequately roast 60 kg of coffee and do four batches in the hour. Whether or not it can is based on the power output of the burner and the ability to modulate airflow.

As a simple test, when commissioning our roaster at Market Lane I did a very short warming period (10 minutes or so), then loaded the roaster with 100 per cent of its rated capacity (15 kg) and roasted it as fast as it could. Our roaster completed the roast in eight minutes on full gas, so I was satisfied that the burner would have sufficient power output for our needs.

When choosing a roaster to purchase, or when comparing models, you can be a bit more scientific about it. It's a good idea to compare the rated burner output on different roasters, specifically in relation to their rated batch size. Author and coffee consultant Scott Rao recommended to me to start with a minimum of 5000 BTU/hr of power per 450 g of coffee to have enough power to sufficiently roast. I applied this 5000 rule to our Probatone 5 kg roaster and discovered that it held true; we had found by tasting and roast duration that just over 4 kg was the maximum batch size that we were happy with (in terms of taste). See the table below for some roaster output comparisons.

Roaster model	Capacity (kg)	Power output (BTU/hr)	Recommended capacity (kg)	Recommended capacity as % of stated capacity
Probatone 5	5	47,390	4.3	86
Probatone 60	60	314,214	28.5	47
Loring S35	35	300,000	27.2	78
'Retro' UG22	22	238,839	21.6	98
G60 from 2007	60	477,680	43.4	72

Applying the 5000 rule to a few different roasters, you can see that there is a great deal of variation in power output per kg of recommended capacity. You can also see quickly that the Probatone 60 is probably underpowered for its stated capacity, but that the rest are pretty close, in that most coffee roasters are happy to use 75 per cent capacity of the machine, but probably not 50 per cent. Scott wasn't suggesting this application to be a perfect rule and I don't want to present it as such – the machines above have very different gas heating mechanisms (especially the Loring) – but it is interesting to use a metric to compare a roaster's power output with its stated capacity.

POWER AND AIRFLOW

Most of the roasters on the previous page have the ability to control the airflow and the heat input separately, with the exception being the Loring. On other roasters with a separate power burner (where the burner is sealed, and the gas and air intake are controlled), the airflow through the roaster is linked to the burner output power. Usually this is because the burner requires the throughput of air to maintain efficient combustion. This can be problematic because at times it might be necessary to maintain a low heat setting, but with an increased airflow throughput. This can be particularly useful at the end of roasts (where the heat input can be very low), or with small batch sizes where slightly decreased airflow might be desirable.

COOLING

Once a batch of coffee is finished roasting, the most common method to arrest the roasting process is to spill the beans out of the drum into the cooling tray – usually a large sieve with agitation arms that pull through room temperature air. The volume, temperature and rate of airflow through the bed of hot coffee determines how quickly the batch of coffee will be cooled. While it's common for roasters to be specified to cool coffee in four minutes, it's equally common to find that this cooling time blows out by several minutes. This is an issue because the longer the coffee takes to cool, the worse it will taste and the less time it will last. I've found that a cooling time of four minutes improves the flavour, with no noticeable improvement in flavour in cooling times less than four minutes. Below are five ways you can reduce the cooling time, from easiest to hardest:

- Clean the cooling tray, underside and piping
- Clean the cooling fan, all the vanes and housing
- Roast smaller batch sizes
- Install a separate cooling fan, or replace the motor with a larger one
- Replace the entire cooling tray with one larger in diameter

Larger commercial roasters often have water quenchers installed inside the drum to flash cool the coffee before spilling it into the cooling tray. I wouldn't recommend using a water quencher to cool the coffee down, however, as there are studies that suggest that the introduction of water can affect the shelf life of the coffee with regards to flavour. That being said, I would suggest that a quencher is still a useful addition to a roaster; in the case of a drum fire, quenching is the safest way to extinguish the flames.

METHODS

As briefly outlined previously, the roasting process is fairly simple, that is if the equipment and coffee you start with is up to scratch. Most problems have their roots in poor equipment, or equipment that is not fit for purpose. Exactly how the coffee is roasted in the drum is referred to as a roast profile, and is a set of data that can be used to compare profiles with one another, with temperature increase shown graphically. Below is a table of the terms used when talking about roasting, and what they mean.

Bean Temperature (BT)	This is taken from the thermocouple inside the drum, closest to the centre of the mass of beans.
Environmental Temperature (ET)	Taken from the thermocouple inside the drum but not in contact with coffee, or in the ducting between the drum and chaff cyclone.
Burner Temperature (BuT)	Taken from the thermocouple that measures the temperature of the heating gas.
Weight loss	The change in coffee weight during the roasting process. Measured as a positive amount (e.g. the roasted coffee is 85 per cent of the weight of the green coffee), or as a negative amount (e.g. the amount of weight lost during the roast is −15 per cent).
First crack	Measured from an audible cue. I recommend starting it from the third audible crack, rather than the very first ones, as I find this eliminates outliers or early starts.
Starting temperature	Normally refers to the bean temperature when the roast commences.
End temperature	Refers to the bean temperature when the roast ends.

continued ➤

Development time	The time from first crack to the end of the roast.
Duration/roast time/roast length	The total roast time, from when the coffee is dropped into the roaster to when it is dropped out of the roaster.
Development Time Ratio (DTR)	A ratio (percentage) of the development time divided by the total roast time.
Rate of Rise (RoR)	The rate at which a particular measurement is changing, usually over a 30-second period. Can refer to the bean, environment or burner temperature.

There are a few general parameters that help produce a good roast instead of a bad one, but for all roasts, one thing is certain: the quality of the roast has to be measured organoleptically (using the sense organs), primarily by tasting. There's no use measuring the weight loss or development time ratio if these factors are not correlated with cup quality. The cup quality is always the target, not the various parameters that help us achieve it. The data collected in particular roasts that taste great should be used later to replicate the results. A lot of tasting is required to determine this.

While every machine and set-up are slightly different, as long as your temperature measuring points are located as described earlier, there are a few general rules that will help in achieving the best taste in the cup.

USE CROPSTER

Cropster (www.cropster.com) is a powerful tool that you can use to track inventory, roast and quality information, and crucially link it back to specific roast profiles. Cropster has improved the quality of our coffee more than any other tool we've tried.

DECREASING RoR

Maintain a decreasing Rate of Rise (RoR) of the bean temperature over the entire roast. For most coffees, a constantly decreasing RoR will produce a better cup than an RoR that decreases then increases. This is another rule that Scott Rao covers in his book *The Coffee Roaster's Handbook*, and it's one that I have generally found to be true, although there are exceptions. The Rate of Rise is calculated by taking the current Bean Temperature and subtracting the Bean Temperature from 30 seconds previously. For example:

	Current temperature	RoR
7:00	180°C	-
7:30	185°C	5°C
8:00	189°C	4°C
8:30	193°C	4°C

As you can see, the RoR can only be applied retrospectively, in that it can only tell you what the rate of change is for the previous 30-second period, rather than an instantaneous change. This can make it challenging to watch during the roast, as the results are delayed. But using the results from a previous roast to predict or pre-empt the RoR results is possible and relatively straightforward.

Maintaining a decreasing RoR towards the end of a roast can be challenging, because the dynamics inside the roaster change a lot at the first crack and the end of the roast. It's further complicated because the RoR at the end of the roast tends be quite low already, sometimes at or below 1°C per minute, and any slight increase in Bean Temperature will show a rise in the RoR value.

ENVIRONMENTAL TEMPERATURE

Using the Environmental Temperature and the RoR of the Environmental Temperature can be useful, and can pre-empt changes in the Bean Temperature.

Opposite is a roast profile of an Ethiopian natural process coffee called Mormora that we recently roasted for espresso. The orange line is the Environmental Temperature (in degrees Celsius), and the blue line is the Bean Temperature. This profile looks fine; there doesn't seem to be any obvious issues with it, but let's have a look at it in more detail.

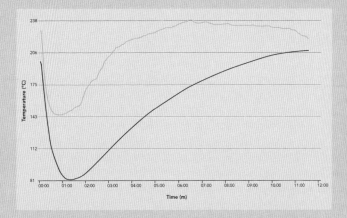

Now we can see the Bean Temperature RoR, also in blue, and the Environmental Temperature RoR in orange. This roast profile still looks okay, but we can see that at about the 9:00 mark, the Bean Temperature RoR almost went into positive value. If we zoom in on this event, we can see how focusing on the Environmental Temperature and RoR might have helped to minimise this effect.

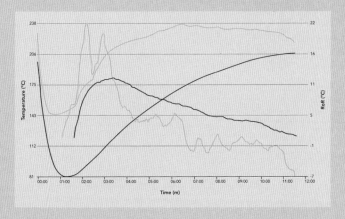

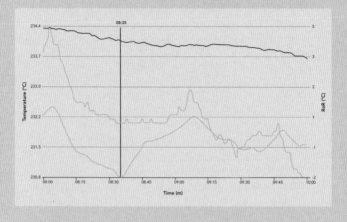

In the two figures above, the blue line represents the Bean Temperature; the top orange line represents the Environmental Temperature; the bottom orange line represents the Environmental Temperature RoR; and the green line at the very bottom shows the gas changes made at particular points. The black line at the 8:35 minute mark of the roast shows an interesting inflection point for the Environmental RoR. It shows a point where there are no gas changes being made, but the Environmental Temperature has started to increase. A gas change was not made until approximately 9:05, and this late change led to a flattening of the Bean Temperature RoR; if left any later, there would have been an increase in the Bean Temperature RoR. If the gas change had been made earlier, when the Environmental Temperature RoR had started to increase at 8:45 or so, the decrease in Bean Temperature RoR probably would have been smoother.

FLAVOUR

The flavour produced by the roasting process is the ultimate determinant of success. The most common faults I taste caused by the roasting process, and their possible solutions, are as follows:

	Flavours produced	Possible solutions
Over-roasting	Ashy, medicinal, rubber, bitter, drying mouthfeel, liquorice	Lower end temperature Shorter roast length
Baking	Dry mouthfeel, lacking sweetness, malt, baking chocolate, flat acidity	Shorter roast length Decrease the BT RoR faster
Under-development	Grassy flavours, lacking sweetness, vegetal notes, grain notes	Higher end temperature Greater starting temperature Lower charge weight
Scorching	Harsh flavours, bitter chocolate	Lower starting temperature Less heat through first crack Higher charge weight

On your particular roaster, you may find that certain roast profiles work for certain origins or types of coffees. I find this approach works about 50 per cent of the time, in that it is useful to start with a profile that worked for a similar coffee, but it's also likely that the new coffee will be different in some way that requires a fresh approach. For example, an approach to roasting a Minas Gerais Brazilian coffee could be to use a relatively low starting temperature, with an early decrease in Burner Temperature when coming into first crack, and a slow increase. This approach would probably not work for a coffee from the Brazilian coffee region of Bahia, however, because despite both these coffees being 'soft' (that is, having a lower density) compared to a Kenyan or Ethiopian coffee, they could still be remarkably different in density.

QUALITY
CONTROL

There are a few crucial elements that every quality-control program requires to be successful. Firstly, you should consider what your goal is in roasting. For example, is it your goal to roast coffee so your wholesale customers can brew espresso to a strength of 10 per cent while tasting great? If so, you will need to include a solubility test in your quality-control program, and ensure all your roast profiles meet this first. Whatever your goals are, you should write them out, and design a program that addresses them. Focusing on a set of goals will free you up to experiment on a range of parameters to find the best-tasting roast profile to fit your needs.

Your quality-control program should take into account how your customers will be consuming your coffee. On pages 100–101, I address the challenge of cities with very hard water – i.e. how using a state-of-the-art water filtration system might make your coffee taste great in the cafe, but what happens when a customer buys it for home and brews the coffee with tap water? There's no easy answer for this, except that you should have an understanding of how your customers will brew the coffee (with domestic equipment and water, etc.) and that your roasting style should accommodate this. One approach might be to periodically check your roasting style with several different types of water solutions, ranging from very hard water to your lab water. Or, using a range of different domestic grinders, try to find a roasting style that suits your own roasting goals and makes your coffee easier to brew for your customers.

Your quality-control program should also specify variables that can affect the coffee flavour when cupping. For example, stipulate what size in grams each sample should be. Is 100 g enough to do espresso tasting? If your chosen cupping ratio is 11 g of coffee to 180 g of water, is it being adhered to? Is the water weighed out? Are all your samples stored in the same place? Are some exposed to more heat than others? Are you evaluating coffees at the same age post-roast? A couple of days testing can make a big difference to the flavour of your coffee.

RETAIL AND WHOLESALE PRICING

Retail pricing should be provided by your wholesaler, so if you are buying roasted coffee from a wholesaler, this pricing structure should be relatively simple. A standard margin for retail products is 30 per cent (for example, a product that was bought from a wholesaler for USD $9 and sold on to retail customers for USD $12 will have a gross profit margin of 25 per cent). This margin should be more if there is wastage of the product involved, and the wholesaler should make provisions for that. In general, the greater the value of the product, the lower the gross profit margin can be: because your fixed costs are the same, you can sell fewer high-value products to make the same dollar amount. In Australia, retail coffee sales are rarely considered more than an afterthought, along the lines of 'let's put a few bags out and hope they sell', and they rarely make up more than 10 per cent of the cafe's revenue. In the United States and the United Kingdom, retail sales are more established, and can generate 40 per cent or more of the cafe's revenue. This is a huge opportunity for low net profit margin businesses that is often overlooked. Cafes run on high costs and low net profit margins, so any advantage you can create over competitors goes a long way.

Theoretical margin calculations can help determine which product lines sit with higher margins, and which sit with lower margins. This can help you make decisions on which prices to increase, if there is a need to. The trouble with margin calculations is that they don't account for a great deal of other expenses that your business incurs day to day. Working out that all your products have a 30 per cent margin does not necessarily mean that you will earn a 30 per cent margin on them, as this does not take into account wastage, loss of stock from damage, staff use, etc. It's better practice to take stock of individual product lines from time to time, to check how close your projected margin is to the actual one.

An interesting case study can be found in the rise of third-party delivery companies such as Uber Eats and Deliveroo. The business model for these companies is simple: they offer delivery services for restaurants in exchange for a percentage of the gross sales (often up to 30 per cent) and a small service charge to the customer. The benefit to their customers is clear: there are now many restaurants offering delivery that previously weren't. The benefits for the restaurants are less clear: they might see a large increase in revenue from delivery sales, but at what cost? The average net profit margin for food and beverage businesses in Australia is just below 8 per cent of gross income[1], so while the increase in product sales and gross sales might be very attractive, if the profit margin on those sales reduces to well below 8 per cent, the increased revenue will have a net negative effect on the profitability of the business as a whole. The lesson from Uber Eats and Deliveroo is clear: if you sell something, make sure you take a portion of it as profit.

Wholesale pricing is more flexible, and often reflects the desire of a company to grow their share of the market, rather than the cost of their product or the cost of production. In theory, the best way to begin a wholesale coffee business would be to work out what costs you would incur to sell your product, then work out whether you can compete on price or quality with other roasters in a given market. If this very simplistic approach was taken more often, there would be a much smaller wholesale market! It's clearly not taken, because prices are commonly discounted to below sustainable rates to grow the market share of companies that offer them. The challenge, of course, is that it's difficult to calculate all the costs incurred in running a wholesale business. Elements that may affect the costs of producing roasted coffee include:

- The structure of the business, whether it's a retail roaster or a wholesaler
- The level of service and training offered at no cost
- Whether machinery is loaned, leased out or sold, and at what margin
- Whether other ancillary products (tea, hot chocolate, disposable cups) are sold or given away

At its most basic, to calculate the product cost, begin with this example:

	Cost ($USD/kg)	Cumulative product cost ($USD/kg)
Green coffee	7	7
Roasting	1.05*	8.05
Packaging	1.05	9.1
Labour	3.5	12.6
Delivery	0.7	13.3
*15% of the coffee is lost in the roasting process		

Obviously, these costs are going to differ wildly between circumstances. The biggest variables are going to be the cost of green coffee to your business, and the labour component cost of roasting it. A team of three people can run a roastery that utilises a 15 kg roaster or a more automated roastery that utilises a 120 kg roaster. Given the output per day will range from 350 kg on a 15 kg roaster all the way up to 3000 kg on a 120 kg roaster, the labour cost will range from USD $5 down to $0.60 per kg.

In summary, it's very important to understand what your costs are, and you should use these costs to determine your selling price. Our industry is filled with businesses and individuals making a loss because they don't understand their costs fully, or they don't have control over them, and this is to the detriment of our industry as a whole.

---

1 The net profit margin in the United States is reported to be lower, at around 6 per cent. Crucially, this reported net profit does not take into account unreported costs, such as cash payments to staff and income being stripped by the owner (cash taken out of the till). I suspect that Australia has a higher net profit margin simply because there is a higher rate of declaring income than the United States, and the main reason for this is that we have a much higher rate of card payments than the US. Card payments are harder to make disappear than cash, so these are generally reported.

BREWING

COFFEE

BREWING COFFEE AT HOME

Brewing coffee can be fun and easy, but a lot of people still find it daunting. I think much of this apprehension is because it's not very common to see coffee brewed, or if it is, it is done behind expensive machinery. A big barrier for people is often the equipment needed to get started, but there are many ways to brew coffee and some of them don't require expensive equipment. At its most basic, coffee is brewed with hot water and then the grounds are separated from the mixture with a filter or by gravity.

EXTRACTION AND STRENGTH

Only a portion of coffee is soluble in water. The most you can dissolve in water is 30 per cent of the weight of ground coffee, but to get the best flavour and balance, around 20 per cent is ideal.

A few things contribute to the rate at which solubles are extracted from coffee:

- Water temperature: a higher temperature will extract more.
- Particle size: a smaller particle size will allow more extraction.
- Agitation: the more the coffee is agitated, the greater the extraction – think of jiggling a teabag.
- Pressure: the pressure under which water is forced through a bed of coffee will impact the level of extraction.

The variable that has the biggest influence, and the one we change most often at Market Lane, is the particle size, or what we call grind size. This is adjusted on grinders by changing the distance between the two burr sets – the closer the burrs are together, the finer the grind.

Coffee particle size is very hard to communicate because it's so difficult to measure, so it's much easier to relate it to other substances we are familiar with. The particle size for plunger-ground coffee is close to the coarseness of rough sand and, at the other end of the spectrum, the particle size for espresso-ground coffee is between table salt and a fine powder. The best way to get started is to ask for an example of grind size from your local roaster and feel the grind size between your fingers to understand the range.

The word 'strong' is used in coffee marketing to mean 'flavourful'. In reality, the strength of a coffee is a measure of the heaviness of the texture of the brew. Or, to put it another way, strength is the weight of the mouthfeel of the coffee.

Strength can be measured by calculating the dissolved solids that are held in the brew, and these solids can make coffee feel heavier or lighter in the mouth. Most people enjoy filter coffee that's at a strength of 1.3–1.4 per cent, and espresso coffee that is 8–10 per cent. This should put into perspective the relative strength of espresso compared to filter coffee.

A common misconception is that the strength of coffee refers to its caffeine content. However, two different varieties of coffee brewed to exactly the same strength (in total dissolved solids percentage) can have very different levels of caffeine.

TYPES OF GRINDERS FOR HOME

Historically, coffee was ground by pounding the beans using a mortar and pestle, similar to the way spices are ground. Nowadays, coffee is ground in three common ways.

ELECTRIC BURR GRINDERS

These are the most common types of grinders. There are two types of electric burr grinders: flat burr and conical burr. The resulting difference between the two is not huge and not easily quantifiable. In general, though, conical-burr grinders are designed for espresso brewing, and flat-burr grinders are used for everything else. Conical burrs create a portion of very fine particles that slow down the rate of espresso extraction, allowing for a stronger brew. They are generally used in domestic grinders because they can be produced more economically, in terms of cost and size; a conical burr has more cutting surface area than a flat burr of the same diameter. Flat-burr grinders tend to produce less variance in particle size, allowing for a more even extraction with a longer brewing time, which is great for filter-coffee brewing or any method in which you can control the steeping time.

Electric-burr grinders can range in price from a few hundred dollars for a small domestic unit up to thousands for a commercial grinder. An electric-burr grinder is highly recommended for simple, successful brewing at home, and there are many options that are of good quality and affordable.

ELECTRIC 'WHIRLY-BLADE' GRINDERS

While these are commonly used for grinding coffee at home, they unfortunately don't do a very good job. The grinder chamber at the top of the grinder contains four blades that spin, slicing up the beans as they do so. There is very little control over the coffee particle size and the grinders tend to pulverise the coffee rather than creating even-sized particles. The low price point makes them an attractive option, but as they grind coffee to a wide range of particle sizes, the coffee will brew with a large range of extractions, resulting in more sour, acidic, bitter and harsh flavours.

HAND GRINDERS

These are simple and effective, with good-quality versions making coffee that rivals expensive electric grinders. The only drawback is that it takes about a minute to grind enough coffee for one cup, compared with only a few seconds using an electric grinder. That said, they are perfect for a small kitchen, or for someone who travels a lot and loves to take coffee with them. Most hand grinders follow a similar design to that of a pepper mill, with a chamber in the top for whole beans, a middle grinding chamber with a fixed outer burr and rotating inner conical burr, and a lower chamber that holds the ground coffee. Look for one that is made from good materials, with steel or ceramic burrs.

OTHER EQUIPMENT

In addition to a grinder, you will need a few extra tools to help you brew your coffee. I've tried to keep this list as short as possible and only outline the essentials, so as not to over-complicate a very simple process. Unfortunately, though, there are many different pieces of equipment you can buy, and new ones appear on the market every year. For example, there is now a machine that can automatically dose coffee out to a fraction of a gram – to the accuracy of a single bean! Now this might be excessive, but the point is that if you're looking for more coffee-brewing 'toys', there are lots out there.

SCALES

Scales are great because they can help you quickly and accurately determine the amount of coffee and water you are using to brew with. For example, instead of having to decant a kettle of boiled water into a measuring pitcher, you can place the whole brewing apparatus on the scales, tare it off and then add the correct amount of water required by weight. When weighing the coffee itself, scales are useful for their accuracy, especially when changing between different types of coffee, which can vary in density. Additionally, if you do even a small amount of baking and cooking at home, a good set of scales will make your life a lot easier.

TIMER

The length of time that your coffee brews will greatly influence the flavour. In the same way that steeping tea for too long can ruin a cup, leaving coffee to brew for too long can have the same effect. So a timer for keeping track of the length of your brew is extremely useful. You don't need anything fancy, though.

KETTLE

Some stovetop kettles are specifically designed to pour water gently when brewing coffee, and while they're not absolutely necessary, they do look great in the kitchen! Whether you have a pouring kettle or an electric kettle, just be sure to not let the water cool down too much after boiling and before brewing.

BREWING ESPRESSO AT HOME

Brewing coffee under pressure allows you to extract a higher-strength coffee in a shorter amount of time. Espresso machines were developed in Italy in the early 1900s so that numerous cups of coffee could be made quickly and to order. They were simple machines that used steam pressure to force hot water through a small amount of coffee. Initially this was done at quite high temperatures and relatively low pressure, but it was soon discovered that using water at a temperature of 90–95°C (195–205°F) yielded a far superior flavour. Brewing at higher pressures also resulted in a sweeter, stronger cup, and so spring-loaded, piston-pressurised machines quickly became the most popular.

STOVETOP PERCOLATORS

The traditional stovetop coffee maker has not changed in design since the 1930s, when the Bialetti Moka Express was widely adopted. It is a simple design with an octagonal aluminium water reservoir as the base, a small basket for holding ground coffee, and a chamber above to hold the brewed coffee. Its mechanism is extremely straightforward: the pot is placed on the stove; the water is heated; and as this happens the pressure inside the base increases to a point where it forces the water upwards through the coffee. This pressure is less than that created by modern espresso machines, or even the mechanical lever espresso machines of the 1920s, but it's enough to create a high temperature, and can extract more strength than is possible without pressure.

The grind size of the coffee should be relatively fine – similar to the size of white sugar or table salt granules. Many people use a very fine grind, similar to espresso or even finer, but I find that a coarser grind reduces the bitterness of the stovetop brew. Many places will recommend a darker roast for this brewing method, but I've found that this is mostly to achieve a strong 'Italian' coffee. If you don't mind a coffee with a little less strength, I would recommend using a lighter roast coffee that will result in a better flavour.

Making stovetop percolator coffee

1. Bring 500 ml (17 fl oz) water to the boil.
2. Rinse the percolator with hot water to warm it up and to ensure it's clean.
3. Fill the filter basket with coffee, ensuring the coffee bed is nice and even and flat, then brush any coffee from the edge of the basket.
4. Fill the base of the pot with the boiled water, up to the height of the small pressure valve. If there is no valve, then fill to about three-quarters full. Place the filter basket into the base and firmly screw down the top.
5. Place the percolator on the stovetop (either gas or electric; induction won't work) over medium heat and open the lid. Because the water was hot to start with, the coffee will start flowing through the top of the stem quite quickly. Once coffee stops flowing from the stem, remove the pot from the heat, close the lid, and enjoy!

If you find your stovetop coffee is too weak, try using a finer grind size, or more coffee in the basket (and the reverse if it's too strong).

ESPRESSO MACHINES

By the 1920s, espresso machines contained electric heating elements, spring-loaded piston levers for pressure, and a steam boiler to heat and texture milk. There have been some developments in espresso machines since then, but surprisingly few. The largest development was the introduction of rotary pumps to produce the pressure required to make espresso, and more recently the introduction of fairly standard engineering equipment, such as the temperature controller PID. These developments have delivered some incremental improvements, but nothing revolutionary as yet.

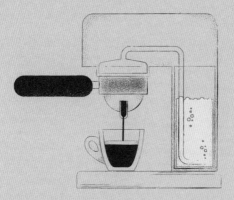

I think it's important to understand a bit about espresso machines and their intended purpose when considering them for use in your home. Some of the drawbacks are:

- They can take a long time to warm up.
- Success is largely driven by the quality of coffee grinder you have (so it needs to be good).
- It takes a fair bit of practice to make a good espresso at home.
- They can take up a lot of space in your kitchen.

It's for these reasons that I don't have an espresso machine at home, and instead have a filter cone (see page 88) and a good grinder. If I wanted a stronger brew than filter coffee at home, I would probably choose a stovetop percolator over an espresso machine.

That said, a lot of people do have an espresso machine at home, so here are a few tips to get the most out of them.

- Start with good-quality coffee and go from there. Low-quality coffee will never taste good, no matter how well it is brewed.

- Make sure the espresso machine and grinder are well cleaned. The biggest source of contamination in espresso coffee is dirty equipment. Be sure to clean the portafilter, basket, shower screen and group head very well before use.

- Ensure the portafilter and espresso machine are thoroughly warmed up before use. Running some hot water from the espresso machine through the empty portafilter can help warm it up more.

- Always grind your coffee fresh and use an amount that is appropriate for the basket size. As soon as coffee is ground, it starts to lose aromatics and flavour. Some machines will require a little more room than others between the top of the coffee bed and the top of the basket – so adjust accordingly. At the very least there should be 3–4 mm (¼ in) of space between the coffee bed and the top of the basket after the coffee is tamped down. In most cases this can be achieved by filling the basket completely, but not overfilling by creating a mound in the basket, before tamping.

- Use a tamper to press down on the bed of coffee. Ensure that the tamper is level and clean. You don't need to press down with a lot of force, just enough to compact the coffee a little.

- Aim to stop your shot at 30 seconds and/or when the shot weighs approximately twice the weight of the ground coffee used. This is called the brew ratio, and it will dictate the strength and flavour of your espresso shot. For example, starting with 18 g (0.635 oz) of ground coffee and using this to brew an espresso that weighs 36 g (1.27 oz) is a brew ratio of 1:2. I would recommend staying within a brew ratio of 1:1.8 and 1:2.3 to get the best balance between flavour and strength. A higher ratio makes a stronger cup, but can result in sourness. A lower ratio will make a weaker cup, but it might have a better flavour. Play around with the ratio as every espresso machine is different.

- Experiment with the brewing time by increasing or decreasing the grind size. A finer grind will create more resistance for your espresso machine, and therefore the shot time will be longer. This works conversely for a coarser grind. Generally, espresso will only taste good if it is brewed between 25 and 35 seconds.

- If making a coffee with milk, use good-quality milk. I recommend using full-cream (whole) milk, as fresh as you can get it, and one that has been through as little processing as possible. Look for certified organic and biodynamic milk and, if you can, avoid milk that's been homogenised or high-temperature treated.

ESPRESSO DRINK RECIPES

Follow the guidelines on the previous pages, and take note of the operating instructions for your espresso machine, because there are many different products out there. The following are instructions on how to construct these particular drinks at home, rather than specific ratios and volumes. Be guided by your cup sizes, and trust your taste to make your own variation on these drinks.

ESPRESSO

The espresso is a small drink designed to be made and consumed quickly. It is also the base of most espresso-brewed milk drinks. A single espresso is usually 15–20 ml (½–¾ fl oz) in volume, and served in a demitasse cup (60 ml/2 fl oz).

DOUBLE ESPRESSO/ LONG BLACK/AMERICANO

The double espresso, as it sounds, is two single-shot espressos. The long black is a double espresso pulled on top of 50–100 ml (1¾–3½ fl oz) hot water. The Americano was so named by Italian baristas pulling very long espressos for American tourists in Europe. It's essentially a very long, long black intended to mimic American filter coffee. It's more commonly brewed now with a double espresso poured on top of 200 ml (7 fl oz) hot water.

MILK ESPRESSO DRINKS

Espresso and hot milk is a great combination. Well-textured milk has a lovely silky mouthfeel and if it's good quality it should taste fresh and sweet, which beautifully complements the strong flavour of espresso coffee. If you like a milky coffee, or a weaker-flavoured coffee, I would recommend using just a single shot of espresso (or even less) in a 200 ml (7 fl oz) cup. If you prefer a strong coffee flavour then I would recommend starting with a double shot of espresso and adding milk, to taste.

Heating milk for espresso drinks using steam has many benefits; the primary ones being that it's very fast – sometimes only taking 15 seconds to heat – and the swirling action of the milk changes the texture of the milk as it warms, making it thicker and more voluminous, resulting in a rich and creamy mouthfeel.

The best temperature to heat milk for espresso drinks is 63–65°C (145–150°F) – hot enough that you can't gulp it down, but still a perfect sipping temperature. There are a few tricks to making silky-textured milk for coffee drinks:

- Always start with fresh milk and a clean milk pitcher. Once milk has been heated and textured, the proteins are structurally different from those of cold milk, and can't be returned to their prior state by chilling the milk again. Texturing previously heated milk will give you a drier, more bubbly result.

- Fill the milk pitcher to about two-thirds full. This gives you the ideal amount for good agitation without running the risk of milk spilling over the side.

- Add air to the milk before it gets hot. Using the steam wand, gently break the surface of the milk to incorporate some air, but only until the milk is warm. Once the milk is above 50°C (122°F) it doesn't incorporate air as well as it does when it's cold – it tends to make the milk bubbly rather than stretched.

- Agitate. I find the best textured milk is created when there is a lot of movement of milk in the pitcher. I aim to create a whirlpool of spinning milk as soon as I start steaming. This agitation creates a similar effect to whipping egg whites, making the milk thicker and beautifully textured.

The end result should be milk that is very glossy in appearance, and when you swirl the pitcher the milk should be slightly thickened, with a consistency similar to pouring cream.

The steam valves on commercial and domestic espresso machines naturally become constricted with old milk as they age, so I recommend getting them serviced regularly to keep the valves performing as they should. The more constricted they become, the harder the boilers have to work to create the same amount of steam pressure, and usually the pressure just dwindles to a point where it is very hard to create great textured milk.

Popular milk espresso drinks include:

Cappuccino – The most famous milk-based coffee drink in the world. The name originated from the dark hazelnut–brown colour of espresso mixed with milk, which resembled the colour of the robes of Capuchin monks. The chocolate sprinkles are a recent addition to the cappuccino, and I consider them optional. It is usually made with a single shot of espresso and quite foamy textured milk in a 150 ml (5 fl oz) cup.

Cortado – A Spanish-named drink; an espresso with about 100 ml (3½ fl oz) of steamed milk added.

Macchiato – An espresso with a very small amount of fresh or steamed milk added.

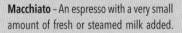

Piccolo – An espresso with 40 ml (1¼ fl oz) of steamed milk added. Also known as a piccolo latte.

Flat white – Essentially the same as a cappuccino, except the milk is textured much more thinly. Well-textured milk for a flat white should be glossy and free from large bubbles. It should be quite thin – the consistency of pouring cream. Brew an espresso into a 150 ml (5 fl oz) cup and fill with thinly textured milk.

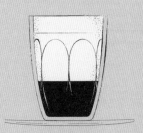

Caffe latte – As the name just means 'milk coffee', there's no strict international definition for what a caffe latte is. In Europe, it can be stovetop-brewed coffee with hot milk, or it can be espresso and steamed milk. In Australia and New Zealand, the standard latte is an espresso in a 220 ml (8 fl oz) glass, topped with textured milk. In the US and UK, lattes are usually larger – from 350 ml (12 fl oz) to 500 ml (17 fl oz) or more!

A WORD ON MILK QUALITY

It's worth noting that the flavour of your milk espresso drink will not only be as good as your espresso, but also your milk. I have gone into more detail about milk quality on page 28, but, essentially, milk production has been increasingly industrialised over the last 50 years, resulting in most commercial milks coming from farms that over-produce milk and factories that create huge lots of bland-tasting product. Where you can, find a local and organic milk producer; seek out farmers' markets and local grocery stores, and ask questions! Milk can have a great range of flavours and styles, so don't settle for supermarket brands because they are convenient.

COLD COFFEE DRINKS

These can be very refreshing and are especially popular in places with hot summers. They can be made with espresso coffee, hot-brewed filter coffee, or they can be brewed with cold water. In cafes, espresso-based iced coffees tend to be the best. Since the coffee is strong, you only have a small volume of hot liquid (about 40 ml/1¼ fl oz) to chill, so you can still brew it fresh and cool it quickly with the addition of ice and milk.

The difficulty associated with quickly chilling hot filter coffee means that cafes have been looking at alternative ways of brewing coffee for cold drinks. One widely adopted method is cold brew, which uses a very high proportion of coffee to water, and a very long steep time, sometimes 24 hours. This allows you to achieve the same strength of coffee brew as you would when using hot water. Cold water does not extract coffee in the same way as hot water does, so the flavour of cold-brew coffee is normally very muted and a little bit chocolatey and malty. I would not recommend cold brew, and instead suggest using espresso or iced pour over for cold coffee drinks.

Iced long black – Three-quarters fill a glass with good-quality ice and cold filtered water, then top with a freshly brewed double espresso. You can adjust the strength by adjusting the amount of cold water you use – 150 ml (5 fl oz) is a good amount to start with.

Iced latte – Three-quarters fill a glass with good-quality ice and milk, then top with a freshly brewed double espresso. If you like your coffee sweeter, add some raw sugar to the hot espresso before mixing it into the cold milk.

Coffee spritz – Three-quarters fill a glass with good-quality ice and tonic water, then top with a freshly brewed double espresso. It sounds like an odd combination, but the quinine in the tonic works really well with the body of the espresso, and makes for a very refreshing drink.

BREWING FILTER COFFEE AT HOME

In this section we'll look at brewing methods that do not use pressure in their brewing. They require less equipment, are generally easier to clean and are ideal to use at home.

For all filter methods, a recipe of approximately 65 g (2¼ oz) of coffee per 1 litre (34 fl oz) of water will suit. You can vary this according to your personal taste, but it's a good starting point for the following brewing methods.

PLUNGER (FRENCH PRESS)

The plunger is one of the simplest and oldest brewing methods. Commonly made from a glass cylinder with a metal stem and mesh filter, plungers come in different sizes, including three-cup (350 ml/12½ fl oz) and eight-cup (1 litre/34 fl oz). You will need to adjust your recipe to suit the size of your plunger.

Equipment: plunger, kettle, scales and timer.

Coffee: the grind should feel like coarse sand between your fingers. You'll need 23 g (¾ oz) of coffee for a three-cup plunger and 65 g (2¼ oz) for an eight-cup plunger.

1. Bring 500 ml (17 fl oz) water to the boil for three cups or 1.25 litres (42 fl oz) to the boil for eight cups.
2. Rinse the plunger glass and filter with hot water to warm it up and to ensure it's clean. Drain.
3. Add the coffee to the plunger glass and fill with 350 ml (12½ fl oz) just-boiled water for three cups and 1 litre (34 fl oz) for eight cups. Pour the water in quickly so it agitates the coffee a little as you pour.
4. Start your timer and let the coffee brew for 1 minute, then give it a good stir. Brew for a further 3 minutes.
5. Slowly push the plunger down as far as it will go, so the plunger is holding the ground coffee firmly on the bottom of the plunger. Now pour and enjoy!

POUR OVER

This method can be made using a variety of coffee makers of different shapes and sizes. Popular brands include Melitta, Hario V60, Bee House and Clever Coffee Dripper, just to name a few. All of these brands work in essentially the same way: they are (or hold) a cone-shaped filter in which ground coffee is placed and then hot water is poured over to brew the coffee. The filter holds back the ground coffee solids, leaving a clear and light-bodied coffee brew to drip through into a cup. This is a very popular method for brewing at home, because it's simple and easy to clean up. Depending on the size of the maker, you can make between one and six cups at a time, but I normally recommend the two-cup size. The following instructions relate to the glass or ceramic drippers that use paper filters.

Equipment: coffee dripper/cone, filter paper, kettle, scales and timer.

Coffee: the grind should be finer than what you would use for a plunger, but coarser than espresso. A helpful measure of the proper grind size is the time it takes to brew, and 3 minutes is a good target. You'll need 30 g (1 oz) of coffee to make two cups.

1. Bring 1 litre (34 fl oz) water to the boil.
2. Fit the filter paper into the cone and rinse the cone and a serving jug with hot water to warm them up and to ensure they're clean.
3. Place the coffee into the filter-lined cone and place the cone on top of your serving jug.
4. Place the jug and cone onto your scales. Pour in enough boiled water to cover all the coffee – about three times the weight of the coffee (in this case about 90 g/3 oz water).
5. Start your timer for 3 minutes, give the coffee and water a good stir and leave to 'bloom' for about 30 seconds (this helps the coffee to degas and rearrange itself into an even bed, encouraging an even extraction).
6. Pour in more boiled water, slowly and in a circular motion, about 150 g (5½ oz) at a time and waiting about 30 seconds between pours, to bring the total amount of water to 500 g (1 lb 2 oz). Aim to finish pouring at the 2:15 minute mark, which will help get you to a total brew time of 3 minutes and 30 seconds as the coffee finishes drawing down.

ICED POUR OVER

Pour over is also a great method to use when making iced coffee. Simply choose the amount you wish to brew, then substitute one-third of the brew water that you would normally use with the same weight in ice. For example, if using 500 g (1 lb 2 oz) water and 30 g (1 oz) of coffee to make an iced pour over, you would use 150 g (5½ oz) of ice, 350 g (12½ oz) hot water and 30 g (1 oz) of coffee.

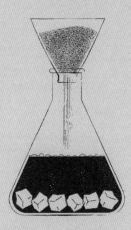

1. Bring 1 litre (34 fl oz) water to the boil.
2. Fit the filter paper into the cone and rinse with hot water to warm it up.
3. Weigh out 150 g (5½ oz) of ice into your serving jug, then place the coffee into the filter-lined cone and place the cone on top of your serving jug.
4. Place the jug and cone onto your scales. Pour in enough boiled water to cover the coffee – three times the weight of the coffee (about 90 g/3 oz water).
5. Start your timer for 3 minutes, give the coffee and water a good stir and leave to 'bloom' for about 30 seconds (this helps the coffee to degas and rearrange itself into an even bed, encouraging an even extraction).
6. Pour in more boiled water, slowly and in a circular motion, about 150 g (5½ oz) at a time and waiting about 30 seconds between pours, to bring the total amount of water to 500 g (1 lb 2 oz). Aim to finish pouring at the 2:15 minute mark, which will help get you to a total brew time of 3 minutes and 30 seconds as the coffee finishes drawing down.
7. Stir the coffee to melt the remaining ice, and serve in a tall glass of ice.

AEROPRESS

Compared with other brewing devices out there, the AeroPress is definitely the new kid on the block. The inventor, Alan Adler of Stanford University (and of Aerobie frisbee fame), developed the AeroPress with the aim of making a high-quality single-cup brewer that could brew coffee quickly. The result is a sort of hybrid between a plunger and a pour over, with a small amount of pressure used to force the brewed coffee through a paper filter. The AeroPress has gained a well-deserved reputation for producing consistently great coffee with minimal fuss. The versatility of this brewer is highlighted by the huge number of different methods that are employed at the World AeroPress Championships (WAC) each year. We have found success with many of these methods from the WAC website, but our favourites are the simplest ones.

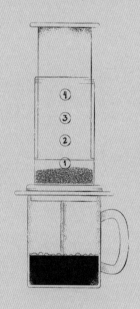

Equipment: AeroPress, filter paper, kettle, scales and timer.

Coffee: Your grind should be the same as you would use for pour over – finer than what you would use for a plunger but coarser than espresso. You'll need 15 g (½ oz) of coffee to make one cup.

1. Bring 500 ml (17 fl oz) water to the boil.
2. Place the filter paper in the filter holder and attach it to the bottom of the AeroPress. Leave the plunger piece to one side for the moment. Place the bottom of the AeroPress on top of a cup and rinse with hot water. Allow to sit for a moment to warm the cup, then tip out the water and sit the cup and AeroPress on top of your scales.
3. Place the coffee into the AeroPress and fill with 200 g (7 oz) boiled water.
4. Carefully place the plunger part into the top of the AeroPress (this will stop the coffee dripping through the filter) and start your timer. After 1 minute, carefully remove the plunger and give the brew a good stir. Leave to brew for a further 1 minute.
5. Gently and slowly push the plunger down until the coffee brew is completely pushed through the paper filter.

To clean the AeroPress, turn it so the filter holder is facing up and remove the plastic filter holder. Slowly press the spent coffee and paper filter into the bin or compost.

BREWING COFFEE FOR CAFES

While the previous chapter provides you with a great start for brewing espresso at home, brewing coffee in a cafe environment allows for a great deal more experimentation and finessing, not just because of the commercial equipment used, but also because of the volume. With repeatability comes consistency, and this allows the cafe barista to more acutely focus on the finer details of espresso extraction. Because of this, I think that cafe-brewed espresso will always be superior to home-brewed espresso, and that is not a bad thing!

WATER

First of all, let's talk about water. Water plays a very important part in coffee brewing, not only through its chemistry and its ability to extract coffee, but also as an ingredient.

Water can make up 98.7 per cent of the brew for filter coffee by weight, and about 90 per cent of black espresso coffee, so any flavour taints or problems with the water will carry through to the final product. Common taints include chlorine, sulphur or metallic flavours from old pipes. It's extremely important to remove any taints before using water to brew coffee, which can be easily done with a simple carbon filter.

Ideal water chemistry for brewing coffee can be a very complicated matter, and one that very few people (myself included) fully understand. Research has found that, in order to achieve the best taste when brewing coffee, there is certainly an ideal mineral composition, pH level and so on when it comes to water, but the challenge is that the composition of water is different everywhere. You'll find differences in the water within different parts of a city, not to mention parts of a country and the world. Generally, there are two methods of water treatment that cafes can choose from: filtration and reverse osmosis plus remineralisation. There are benefits and drawbacks for each method, outlined below.

Carbon filter	
Pros	Cons
Cheap	Not customisable
No waste water created	Does not change overall hardness of water
Small physical footprint	
Low carbon footprint	

Reverse Osmosis and Remineralisation	
Pros	Cons
Water is completely customisable	Can waste a lot of water
Works for hard and soft water	Uses power
Allows water standardisation across multiple locations	Expensive to buy and expensive to run

The first step in deciding whether or not you need reverse osmosis is to do a water test (these kits are readily available). Test for hardness, pH and alkalinity, and if any of these are way outside of the Specialty Coffee Association (SCA) guidelines (hardness between 75-250 mg/L, pH between 6.5-7.5 and alkalinity at or near 40 mg/L), then you should seriously consider reverse osmosis. That said, in Melbourne, where Market Lane is based, our water is a little too soft (around 50 mg/L in hardness), but our coffee tastes and extracts well enough for us to use carbon filters quite happily.

Another big consideration in deciding whether to treat your water is how your retail coffee will taste when consumed at home by your customers. If you are roasting and brewing with perfect water in the roastery and cafe, but your customers are brewing with water that is extremely strong and full of minerals, your roasting style will probably not taste all that good in their homes. I don't know what the answer to this is, but probably the best practice is to start with good water in your roastery and cafe, then test your roasts with a range of different waters. If nothing else, this will give you an indication as to how your coffee is being consumed outside of the cafe or roastery.

GRINDING AND EXTRACTION

Many of the basics concerning grinding and extraction are covered earlier in the Brewing at Home chapter. In this chapter, I will go into more detail, both for filter-coffee brewing and espresso-coffee brewing, and how they relate to coffee brewing in cafes.

ELECTRIC BURR GRINDERS

These are the most common types of grinders used in cafes, shop roasters, and as good domestic grinders. There are two types of burr grinders – flat burr and conical burr. The resulting difference between the two is not huge and not easily quantifiable. In general, though, conical burr grinders are designed for espresso brewing and flat burr grinders for everything else. Conical burrs create a portion of very fine particles that slow down the rate of espresso extraction, allowing for a stronger brew. Conical burrs are generally used in domestic grinders because they can be produced more economically, in terms of cost and size – a conical burr has more cutting surface area than a flat burr of the same diameter. Flat-burr grinders tend to produce less variance in particle size, allowing for a more even extraction with a longer brewing time, which is great for filter-coffee brewing or any method in which you can control the steep time.

Electric burr grinders can range in price from a few hundred dollars for a small domestic unit up to thousands for a commercial grinder. Recently, there have been some improvements to the design of grinders, with two goals: to improve usability (i.e. quickly deliver a very specific dose of ground coffee) and to decrease the grind size distribution. To that end, improvements have been made in the following areas:

- Temperature control. The temperature at which coffee is ground affects the grind size distribution. Recent research seems to conclude that the higher the temperature of the burrs and burr housing, the greater the grind size distribution. And while there have been mechanisms to cool grinders for many years, only recently have they gotten to a stage where they markedly improve the performance of grinders, either by modulating the speed of the fans, or by having enough airflow to affect the burr housing temperature.

- Burr speed. Recent research also seems to conclude that the lower the burr speed, the lower the grind size distribution. The challenge with low burr speed (measured in revolutions per minute, or RPM) is that the motors in these low RPM grinders require a very high torque to actually grind the coffee. The more speed, or RPM, that a motor has, the less power it needs to to grind the coffee. Conversely, the less speed a motor has, the more power is required. Because it's cheaper to produce high RPM and low torque motors, these grinders are much more prevalent and popular.

Delivering an accurate dose of coffee quickly is another challenge that grinder manufacturers are facing. They tend to diverge into two camps, in terms of which direction their research and production will take: gravimetric or time-based dosing. Time-based dosing is a simpler way of producing fairly accurate results, and the Mazzer Robur-E is a good example of this type of grinder. When a button is pressed on this grinder, it activates its motor for a preset time (2.5 seconds, for example), to deliver a dose of ground coffee to approximately your specifications. The drawback of this is chiefly that, once the temperature of the grinder is stable, the dose of coffee varies – and some grinders are better than others – by +/- 1 g. In a cafe setting, this would mean that a grinder set to dose 18 g of coffee would have a variance of 17.5–18.5 g. In my experience, this variance is a little outside what is acceptable, but only by a small amount of 0.2 g per dose. I don't think that a variance of 17.7–18.3 g has a large impact on the cup taste. The benefit of time-based grinders is that they are fast; most new Mazzer Robur-E grinders with new but broken-in burrs will grind 18 g of coffee in 2.5 seconds.

I haven't had much experience with gravimetric grinders, or grinders that use scales to dose coffee, but have heard anecdotally that they are slow – that they take 10–15 seconds per dose to weigh and grind in the portafilter. I will go over the benefits and drawbacks on page 109, but I'll say here that gravimetric grinders are most likely what will be used in the future, though currently they are too slow for good customer service.

STRENGTH AND EXTRACTION

Strength can be measured by calculating the dissolved solids that are held in the brew, and these solids can make coffee feel heavier or lighter in the mouth. Most people enjoy filter coffee that's at a strength of 1.3–1.4 per cent, and extraction ranges of 18–22 per cent of ground coffee. Strength of coffee can be measured using a Total Dissolved Solids (TDS) meter, but more commonly and accurately refractometers are used. They measure the deflection of a laser beam shot through liquid coffee, and this is used to calculate the amount of dissolved solids in a brew (as compared to the '0' base of distilled water)[1].

Once the strength is determined, this can be used to work out the extraction yield. To calculate manually:

Extraction yield = (brewed coffee [in g] × TDS%) ÷ initial ground coffee (in g).

So: extraction yield = (448 g brewed coffee × 1.4%) ÷ 30 g ground coffee = 0.21 (448 × 0.014) ÷ 30 = 0.21

The extraction yield is 21%.

This extraction yield percentage is a big determinant in the flavour of the brew. Low extraction yields tend to taste sour and grassy, and high extraction yields tend to taste bitter and have a dry mouthfeel. There's some speculation, especially recently, that the higher the extraction yield the better the flavour, but I haven't found that reflected in the cup. It may be the equipment, water or coffee that I'm using, but I find any extraction yields over 23 per cent to taste too bitter to be enjoyable. Certainly, increasing the yield as high as your palate allows is a good thing; all the recipes we talk about only use a small portion of the overall weight of the coffee, yet we buy it all! We may as well try and give our customers the best value for money and extract as much from the coffee as we can.

The extraction of coffee is, by its nature, assumed to be an average. If you read a 21 per cent extraction, there's no way to know whether a portion of the ground coffee used had an extraction rate of 30 per cent, and the remaining extracted at a lower 15 per cent, or whether the entire dose of ground coffee was extracted evenly. This poses a lot of questions, but not a lot of answers, unfortunately. It's possible to taste this unevenness in the extraction, but it's not completely reliable. For example, a grassy taste in the coffee might be an uneven extraction, or it might be very fresh green coffee. An uneven extraction can be caused by an uneven roast, but more commonly it's caused by uneven grinding.

FILTER COFFEE EXTRACTION

Brewing filter coffee in cafes is now largely done on automatic machines, called batch brewers. These can be anywhere from 1 litre to 24 litres, though the most common sizes used in cafes are 3–6 litres. Depending on the manufacturer, these machines can have a range of features that determine the extraction of the coffee, such as pulse wetting, bypass and bloom timing. I won't extrapolate too much on these settings because they vary greatly from model to model. Crucially, one of the principles of well-brewed coffee is forgotten in most cafes when serving bulk-brewed coffee: that it should be brewed fresh.

---

1 The method that is used to measure the coffee brew is often overlooked, and can lead to misleading results. I recommend doing the following each time to take a consistent measurement:

1. Clean the refractometer with an alcohol swab, allow to dry and calibrate with room temperature distilled water.

2. Thoroughly stir the freshly brewed coffee.

3. Take approximately 5 ml (¼ fl oz) of the brewed coffee and drop it onto a clean, cold saucer.

4. After one minute, pipette five drops of the cooled coffee onto the refractometer and take three readings over one minute. The average of the readings should be used as the coffee strength.

5. Once the readings have been taken, wipe the refractometer dry, then clean with an alcohol swab.

With the exception of the United States, most of the markets around the world do not have a high enough turnover of filter coffee to warrant brewing a few litres at a time. In Australia, the virtues of 'batchy' (Australian slang for batch-brewed) are extolled to customers who are told it's more consistent and 'better extracted'. Unfortunately for our customers, I think the benefits are overstated, and premature. Of course, if there was a high turnover of bulk-brewed coffee, then there would be a chance that it could be good, but the usual scenario for me is disappointing. Half the time I order a batch-brewed coffee, it tastes completely stale and undrinkable, and the other half I am informed that the cafe has just run out of brewed coffee and there is a 10-minute wait for the new batch. The point of the story is to brew as much coffee as you can sell in half an hour – and no more!

The principles of filter coffee extraction are not much more complicated than brewing filter coffee at home (see page 92) – the aim is to extract between 19 and 22 per cent of the weight of the ground coffee into the brew, so that the strength is around 1.4 per cent Total Dissolved Solids (TDS). Most of the issues with filter coffee extraction occur when you are unable to brew within these specifications. This could be due to:

- Dull grinder burrs
- Water chemistry or temperature outside the Specialty Coffee Association's (SCA) recommendations[1]
- Defects in roasting (for example, over-roasting will cause a high extraction and under-roasting will cause a low extraction)
- Inadequate recipe selection
- Uneven extraction due to brewing method or technique

ESPRESSO EXTRACTION

Espresso extraction follows the same principles as filter extraction, although traditionally there has been a big difference in the way that coffee is ground when ground for espresso. The one large difference is in the way coffee grinder burrs are designed: espresso burrs are traditionally designed to produce a bi-modal particle size, meaning that 60–70 per cent of the ground coffee particles are one size (approximately 200µm in diameter), 20 per cent are a much smaller size (called 'fines', which are approximately 40μm in diameter) and the remainder are spread across the total particle size distribution.

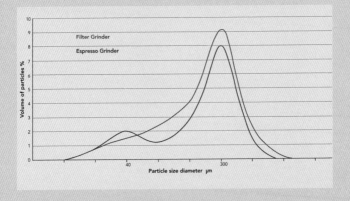

The smaller particles, the fines, serve the purpose of restricting the flow of water through the bed of coffee. This slowed extraction rate helps increase the strength of the espresso brew.

As well as the factors influencing the extraction rate that are listed above, there are a few more to consider when brewing espresso. Your tamping base should fit snugly in the portafilter basket, but not so snugly that a vacuum effect is created when you remove the tamper. This sucks the puck clear of the basket and can cause channelling. I've found 58.3 mm to be the maximum useful diameter for VST baskets. Tamping pressure also impacts extraction, and can now be measured, or checked at least, using the very useful PuqPress automatic tamper. PuqPress can apply 10–30 kg of consistent pressure down onto your puck[2].

1   https://sca.coffee/research/coffee-standards/

2   Interestingly, this tool has highlighted the effect of different distribution techniques used by other baristas I work with. Some baristas distribute the coffee by tapping on the forks of the grinder, others do a 'chop' distribution by tapping the portafilter near the handle with the side of their hand (preferred) while holding it at an angle. Because the previously wildly inconsistent tamping has been eliminated, baristas who use the chop find that it creates more resistance in the ground coffee bed when compared to not distributing at all, or doing a tapping distribution.

The higher the pressure setting, the more densely the coffee will be packed down, and the harder the espresso machine will have to work to extract the coffee. So I recommend choosing a high setting (we use 30 kg), thus allowing the PuqPress to restrict the flow of coffee. Normally, manual light tamping can be more prone to channelling than harder manual tamping, but I haven't found this to extend to PuqPress tamping, either for hard (30 kg) or light (10 kg) tamping.

For Mazzer Robur-E grinders, we've found that keeping the hopper full, or at least half full, keeps the extraction percentage as high as possible. I do not know why, but when the hoppers fall below one-quarter full, the extraction percentage tends to fall by 0.5 per cent, depending on the coffee.

Cleaning and servicing the grinders is also very important. As the grinders are used, hot oil residue from the coffee begins to cake up inside the grinding chamber, and after a usage cycle of 50 kg, there is a noticeable change in the coffee taste. Most notably, the mouthfeel becomes a lot thinner and unbalanced, plus the sweetness and the acidity become thinner and less appealing. I think a lot of taste problems are caused by the increased temperature of the grinding housing. For a cafe using up to 30 kg per week through one grinder, you should be taking apart and cleaning the burr housing to free it of any residual coffee at least once a week. A grinder that hasn't been cleaned in a while can reduce the extraction yield by 1–2 per cent.

The cutting blade of grinders also becomes dull after being used. Each manufacturer recommends a different duty cycle for their burrs, but the most common espresso grinders (Mythos One and Robur) both have a recommended duty cycle of 800 kg before needing to be changed. Probably the most scientific way to determine whether burrs are dull is to look for a change in the extraction yield of the coffee, but I haven't found this method all that effective. For one, even burrs halfway through their duty cycle will not perform as well as fresh burrs, so there is no way of knowing if you are replacing burrs prematurely. I've found the most useful metric is the time the grinder takes to grind a dose; for example, if it normally takes 2.5–2.8 seconds to grind a dose, and the time starts to increase to above three seconds, then the burrs are probably past their effective lifespan.

EFFICIENCY CONSIDERATIONS

Getting bogged down in the technical detail of brewing espresso can make you forget about the most important thing in the cafe – customers! Espresso machines allow us to brew coffee really quickly, and customers expect that their coffee will be served quickly. It sounds intuitive, but it often seems like it's forgotten in specialty coffee that the faster you serve individual customers, the more people you can serve each hour.

While gravimetric grinders are probably the way of the future, I haven't had much experience with them because they're slow. They can take between 10–15 seconds per dose to weigh and grind in the portafilter. Which, for a fast-paced cafe, just won't do. At the rate of 10–15 seconds per dose, a two-group machine would keep up with the grinder easily, and coffee would come out at a maximum rate of one per minute. Time-based grinders (such as the Mazzer Robur-E) can have a dose ground in 2.5 seconds, but more importantly, the portafilter weighed, dose ground and dose adjusted in 8–9 seconds. At this rate, one Robur-E can utilise a four-group espresso machine.

Sharp burrs are vital for getting the most out of your coffee, but they also improve the time efficiency of espresso making. Dull burrs can increase the time it takes the grinder to grind the beans, sometimes increasing the grind time by 50 per cent.

Choosing an appropriate drinks menu will also help to make your barista team more efficient. Do you have several drink menu items that overlap or double up? Cutting down your menu to the bare minimum will save time for your baristas when it comes to drink preparation, ordering and waste. For example, only offer one milk alternative at a time, and only one of each herbal, green or black tea at a time. While customers will tell you that they want choice, there is only a certain amount of choice that is ever considered – large menus distract customers and they enjoy the drink they choose less[1].

A lot of considerations also go into designing the layout of a cafe in terms of efficiency. Designing the layout for a cafe is one of the only times that it is very safe to assume there will be growth in your business. The downside of designing a cafe that can make 1000 drinks per day is that the capital cost of the fit-out will be marginally higher than the capital cost of a cafe that has a lower capacity. But this is usually not a great cost compared to limiting the growth of the cafe, or trying to retroactively increase the capacity for it. So start with a three-group machine, and where there's space (and capital allowance), choose a four-group machine. It's tempting to increase capacity by adding an additional machine to a space, and while this can increase the amount of drinks you can make in an hour, it also means an increase in staff costs for running an additional work area.

Consider the layout of the cafe from the perspective of your customers: what they will see when they walk in; if they will easily find the menu; and where to place their order. This will help them use the space efficiently. But also consider how the layout of the cafe affects how your employees will move through the space while working and serving customers. Are they crossing paths a lot? Are there bottlenecks behind the service counter? I have found that laying out a cafe production space so that staff need to move as little as possible creates the best working environment and the most efficient one. Think about all the possible orders that come in and how they will be made by your employees; this will help you consider where docket printers should be placed, and where the drink pass should be.

1 S. Iyengar, Sheena and Lepper, Mark. (2001). *When Choice is Demotivating: Can One Desire Be Too Much of a Good Thing?* Journal of Personality and Social Psychology.

DRINKS RECIPES
FOR CAFES

Without initially carefully considering drink sizes and recipes, implementing more choices for your menu can complicate it, and cause inconsistencies in pricing and margin. In Australia, this tends to happen with drink recipes relating to takeaway coffee sizes compared to dine-in drink sizes, and the strength of both of these. Takeaway coffees tend to be larger in volume, and presumably that's so customers can drink them on the go, but outside of that, I haven't heard any persuasive arguments for it – it's a convention that has stuck around. Regardless, matching the strength of your dine-in coffees with your takeaway coffees will mean that your customers will be choosing between size only, and not size and strength. This presents a challenge because using a separate recipe for takeaway and dine-in is impractical, and impossible if you offer more than one espresso coffee at a time. The choice is to match the sizes equally, or do multiples of one recipe. For example:

	Split 36 g shot	Full 36 g shot
5 oz dine-in	18 g espresso	-
10 oz takeaway	-	36 g espresso
6 oz dine-in	18 g espresso	-
12 oz takeaway	-	36 g espresso
8 oz dine-in	-	36 g espresso
8 oz takeaway	-	36 g espresso

To develop a drink recipe from scratch, begin with your preferred milk, coffee and cup, then choose the ratio of the espresso to milk that you think would best suit your customers. To do this, brew four double espressos into the same vessel and mix it well. Steam enough milk to fill three cups, then select a few combinations. For example, for a 6 oz cup, try:

- 15 g espresso/90 g milk
- 18 g espresso/90 g milk
- 21 g espresso/90 g milk

If your favourite is the 15 g/90 g combination, then you should split a double shot espresso 30 g beverage weight from a 15 g ground coffee dose in a VST 15 g basket. If your favourite is the 21 g/90 g combination, then you should split a double shot espresso 42 g beverage weight from a 20 g ground coffee dose in a VST 20 g basket[1]. From here, you should choose your takeaway cups, and ensure that the recipe, or double the recipe, works for the cup size you have chosen. Alternatively, you can begin the process with the takeaway cup size, then choose a dine-in cup size.

Once you've established a good espresso-to-milk ratio, the differences between coffee drinks becomes a matter of milk texture. I've found the best way to measure how thickly milk has been textured is by weighing the milk that you add to the espresso. As an indication, milk steamed for an 8 oz[2] takeaway cappuccino will weigh 160 g, and milk steamed for an 8 oz flat white will weigh 180 g. It's really difficult to standardise the amount a drink should be textured without having clear guidelines such as these.

Ultimately, the decisions you make will be due to a great number of factors, such as local precedents and efficiency considerations, but the important thing is to be confident and clear in the choices that you make for your customers. In my experience, customers respond really well to a business that has a clear voice and message, and is one that can be relied upon.

---

1 The baskets are designed to get the most out of the coffee, and the head room space in the basket is a major consideration, so it's best not to deviate too far from the stated use capacity, +/– 1 g of the basket size capacity rating.

2 Disposable cup sizing is almost universally named incorrectly. For example, most '8 oz' paper cups actually hold 265 ml (9 fl oz). Be careful when creating recipes and don't base the volume on the name of the cup – check the volume with a set of scales and water.

TO CONCLUDE

In reading this book, I hope you have found some helpful suggestions for and guidelines to navigating the coffee industry, whether you are a home brewer or looking to start a cafe or roastery. The most special part about this industry is its ability to connect people across the world, from coffee-producing countries like Ethiopia and Kenya, to coffee-consuming cities like New York and Melbourne. There are so many hands that touch this special product, and so many stories to tell along its journey. I hope you can be a part of it too.

INDEX